The Sugar Disease:
DIABETES

Other Books by the Silversteins

ALCOHOLISM
ALLERGIES
CANCER
EPILEPSY
HEART DISEASE

CELLS: BUILDING BLOCKS
   OF LIFE
CIRCULATORY SYSTEMS
THE DIGESTIVE SYSTEM
THE ENDOCRINE SYSTEM
THE EXCRETORY SYSTEM
EXPLORING THE BRAIN
THE MUSCULAR SYSTEM
THE NERVOUS SYSTEM
THE REPRODUCTIVE SYSTEM
THE RESPIRATORY SYSTEM
THE SENSE ORGANS
THE SKELETAL SYSTEM
THE SKIN

ANIMAL INVADERS
A STAR IN THE SEA
A WORLD IN A DROP OF
   WATER
LIVING LIGHTS
THE LONG VOYAGE
MAMMALS OF THE SEA
UNUSUAL PARTNERS

CATS: ALL ABOUT THEM
GERBILS: ALL ABOUT THEM
GUINEA PIGS: ALL ABOUT
   THEM
HAMSTERS: ALL ABOUT THEM
RABBITS: ALL ABOUT THEM
RATS AND MICE

THE CHEMICALS WE EAT
   AND DRINK
THE CODE OF LIFE
GERMFREE LIFE
THE LEFT-HANDER'S WORLD
LIFE IN THE UNIVERSE
METAMORPHOSIS: THE
   MAGIC CHANGE
THE ORIGIN OF LIFE
SLEEP AND DREAMS
SO YOU'RE GETTING BRACES:
   A GUIDE TO ORTHODONTICS

CARL LINNAEUS
FREDERICK SANGER
HAROLD UREY

APPLES
BEANS
ORANGES
POTATOES

The Sugar Disease:
DIABETES

by Dr. Alvin Silverstein
and Virginia B. Silverstein

With an Introduction by
Charles Nechemias, M.D., Consulting Editor

J. B. Lippincott
New York

U.S. Library of Congress Cataloging in Publication Data

Silverstein, Alvin.
  The Sugar Disease: Diabetes

  Includes index.
  SUMMARY: Discusses the symptoms of diabetes, its history, causes,
diagnosis, treatment, and implications for the future of current research.
  1. Diabetes—Juvenile literature. [1. Diabetes] I. Silverstein, Virginia B., joint author. II. Title.
RC660.S558   616.4'62   78-11631
ISBN-0-397-31844-8

9 8 7 6 5 4 3 2

For Marguerite P. Fisher

Acknowledgments

The authors would like to thank Mrs. Nancy Mann of the Juvenile Diabetes Foundation and Dr. Charles Nechemias of The Mount Sinai Hospital and School of Medicine for their careful reading of the manuscript, their many helpful comments and suggestions, and their enthusiastic encouragement.

Contents

Introduction

Diabetes represents a national health problem of increasing importance and interest. An estimated ten millior Americans have the disease, and it is responsible for about three hundred thousand deaths per year in the United States, making it the third leading cause of death—behind only heart disease and cancer. Moreover, its incidence is increasing steadily; more than six hundred thousand new cases are diagnosed every year. In spite of these impressive statistics, diabetes remains a disease about which most people know very little beyond the vague notion that it has something to do with sugar. Furthermore, most people who do know about diabetes think that, since the discovery of insulin and the introduction of antidiabetic pills, the disease can be cured, and presents no problems more serious than the need to avoid excessive consumption of sugar and to take one's medication regularly. In actual fact, nothing could be further from the truth!

Many books have, of course, been written about diabetes; some of them are included in the list of further sources of information at the end of this volume. Most of them, however, are what I like to call "how to" books—manuals of instruction and education for the diabetic patient and his or her family. In this present volume, Dr. Alvin Silverstein and Virginia B. Silverstein have written a "what is" book, telling the reader what diabetes is all about; what may cause it; what happens to the body when it occurs; what treatment is available; what the treatment can accomplish, and, more importantly, what it cannot; and much more. Although this book is not primarily intended for the diabetic patient, the young diabetic and his or her family and friends can obtain much interesting information from it—information that should provide a helpful background to the details of management of his or her particular case. More importantly, the young reader with no immediate connection to diabetes, for whom this book is intended, will find it an interesting and informative introduction to a fascinating and troublesome disease.

Of special interest to many young people should be the chapter on frontiers of diabetes research. In almost no other field of medicine has there been so much investigative research along so many different lines in the past few years. The authors have accomplished no mean feat in highlighting some of the more important areas of this exceedingly complex research activity in simplified and lucid terms.

What we have here, then, is a readable—and understandable—book about a major health problem—a book that should be of interest to all intelligent young people, whether or not they have any personal connection with diabetes. Perhaps some of them will be inspired by the challenges that this disease presents to involve themselves in the search for new knowledge about this age-old disorder. One may hope that from the ranks of readers of this book will come the future scientists who will, at long last, unravel the secrets of diabetes and discover its cure.

Charles Nechemias, M.D.
Assistant Clinical Professor of Medicine
The Mount Sinai School of Medicine
  of the City University of New York

Assistant Attending Physician for Diabetes
  and Physician to the Prenatal Diabetes Clinic
The Mount Sinai Hospital, New York

The Sugar Disease

Jackie Robinson, the first black baseball player to break into the major leagues, was an all-time superstar. For ten years his sparkling play delighted fans all over the world. But very few people knew that for half his big-league career, Jackie was playing with a dark shadow hanging over his future. When he was only thirty-three, Jackie Robinson discovered he had diabetes.

At first Jackie and his doctors were able to keep his disease under good control, and it hardly bothered him at all. But as the years went by, problems appeared. First an old knee injury began to trouble him. He had hurt his knee in one of his daring slides into stolen bases; later he developed an infection in the knee. Doctors treated it with antibiotics, but it just wouldn't heal. Instead, the bacteria multiplied and spread through his body—he nearly died before the infection was finally brought under control. And Jackie's troubles continued. His diabetes affected his nerves and blood vessels and caused burning pains in his legs; because of this, he eventually had to give up playing golf. Tiny blood vessels in his eyes began to bleed. Though doctors fought the damage with the newest techniques of laser surgery, Jackie lost the sight first of one eye, then of the other. Three heart attacks struck within four years, and the last one killed him at the age of fifty-three. The heart of a great athlete had stopped, but the real cause of his death was diabetes.

Diabetes is the third leading killer in the United States. It is mainly a disease of the middle-aged and old, but it can also strike young adults, teenagers, and children. (The earliest cases ever recorded appeared in a sister and brother. The girl first became diabetic at the age of four months, and later her baby brother was diagnosed when he was only nine days old.) Diabetes kills thousands directly. But it is also responsible for the deaths of many more who, like Jackie Robinson, seem to have died from heart disease or some other cause.

Diabetics may suffer from many serious complications. High blood pressure, kidney failure, blindness, nerve damage, and an inability to fight off infections bring misery to many diabetics and may shorten their lives. Altogether, diabetes and its complications account for about three hundred thousand deaths in the United States each year. About five million Americans are known to suffer from this disease, and medical specialists suspect that as many as five million more may have diabetes without knowing it. More than six hundred thousand new cases are diagnosed each year. The National Commission on Diabetes, which reported to Congress in 1975, said that the disease costs the nation five and a half *billion* dollars each year in the expenses of caring for diabetics, and in their lost earnings.

All these dismal statistics might seem to paint a hopeless picture. Yet we already know a great deal about diabetes, and some exciting research now going on in laboratories and medical centers promises to reveal much more in the very near future. We do have means of treating the disease that permit many diabetics to live happy, normal lives. For example, we have a colleague who asked us a few years ago to translate the words, "My medicine is in the refrigerator. May I have it, please?" into Russian for him, so he could ask the hotel clerk for his insulin during a summer trip to the USSR. Or think about the words of a retired schoolteacher friend of ours. Hearing that we were writing a book about diabetes, she wrote us, "I have been a diabetic for twenty-five years. I have given insulin to myself, my youngest brother, and my mother, and still consider diabetes the 'best' and easiest chronic disease to cope with. Count your calories, keep on the go, and have an interest in life, and things won't be so bad. I have never had time to worry about my condition."

How can there be so much variation? How can the same disease be a disaster for some and a mere nuisance for others? Doctors who treat diabetics and scientists who study the disease now suspect that the answer to this riddle may be that diabetes is not a single disease. They think there may be a number of different conditions, all of which share a single striking symptom: the body is unable to use sugars properly, to turn them into the energy needed for life's activities. Therefore, extra sugar builds up in the blood, and may spill over into the urine.

Thus far, the treatment of diabetes has been aimed mainly at treating the basic sign of the disease—the high blood sugar—because its causes have been unknown. As a result, so far we have been able only to *control* diabetes. But now researchers are beginning to find clues to the causes of diabetes. With this new knowledge, hope is growing that true *cures* will be found.

What Is Diabetes?

The name *diabetes* comes from a Greek word meaning "a siphon." Ancient Greek physicians observed one of the most striking symptoms of the disease: people with uncontrolled diabetes usually have a constant, urgent thirst. Though they drink huge quantities of liquids, the fluid seems to run right through them, as water runs through a siphon, for they also have a continual need to urinate. Indeed, it often seems that more fluid comes out than went in.

Later, a second part, *mellitus,* was added to the name of the disease. Mellitus comes from a Latin word meaning "honey," and this description was added because some physicians noticed that flies were attracted to the urine of diabetics, just as flies were attracted to honey. When other physicians tried tasting the urine, they discovered that it was sweet. Most people today just talk about "diabetes," but physicians prefer to use its more precise, full name— diabetes mellitus. In this way they avoid confusion with another, very much rarer disease called diabetes insipidus, in which great quantities of urine are also produced, but in which the urine does not contain sugar.

Many people first discover they have diabetes when a routine medical checkup shows sugar in the blood or urine. They may have such mild cases that no symptoms have shown up at all; all they have is that telltale trace of sugar. Perhaps their sugar tests are positive only at times of great stress, such as during an infection or during pregnancy, and afterward everything seems to go back to normal. Such cases are examples of *latent diabetes* (the condition is "hidden," but may crop up in a more serious form later) or *chemical diabetes* (the person has no symptoms, but there are signs of something wrong in the body's chemistry). Usually all a person with latent diabetes needs to do is eat a sensible diet, get plenty of exercise, and have regular checkups to make sure the condition has not progressed. These are good health rules for anyone.

In some cases, a diabetic condition may be quite serious by the time it is correctly diagnosed. *Juvenile diabetes,* which strikes mainly children, teenagers, and young adults, may develop quite suddenly. The person may feel fine, and then, with hardly any warning, he or she falls so seriously ill that emergency hospitalization may be necessary.

Juvenile diabetics account for only about 10 to 20 percent of the total diabetic population. The far more common forms of *maturity-onset diabetes* usually strike people after the age of thirty-five or forty—and then strike mainly people who are overweight. The probability of getting diabetes roughly doubles with each decade of life, and with each 20 percent of excess weight.

Maturity-onset diabetes usually develops gradually, with plenty of warning signals. But a person may overlook some of the symptoms or think they are due to something else. Reaching for that extra bottle of Coke, one might think, "It certainly is hot today!" A person with a sudden need to urinate more than usual might pass it off with the thought, "It must have been that soup I had for dinner," or "I shouldn't have had that extra glass of milk before bedtime." Even in children, the early signs and symptoms of diabetes may be misinterpreted. If a child suddenly begins wetting the bed, his or her parents are more likely to wonder about emotional problems or spank the child for disobedience than to suspect diabetes. But taken together, the symptoms of diabetes spell out a very clear warning message. Since each of us has about one chance in five of developing diabetes at some time in life, it is a message we should all learn to read.

Here are some of the important warning signs of diabetes:

Frequent urination, producing large amounts of urine.
Extreme thirst (to replace the fluids lost in the urine).
Weakness, listlessness, easy tiring (because the body cannot use sugar for its energy needs effectively enough).
Constant hunger (to replace the food materials lost in the urine).

Loss of weight (because more food materials are being
lost than can be replaced).
Itching in the genital area (due to irritation from the
sugar in the urine).

Some other symptoms that may develop as complications of diabetes are:

Skin disorders, such as frequent boils and infections;
slow healing of wounds.
Blurring of vision and other vision problems.
Pain, numbness, or tingling in the legs and feet.

Who gets diabetes? Different forms of the condition can affect people of all ages, from tiny babies up
to the very old. It strikes both sexes, but women are
more likely to be diabetic than men. Women who
have had a lot of children and those who have had
unusually large babies (weighing ten pounds or more
at birth) seem to face a special risk. People who have
relatives with diabetes (especially the maturity-onset
type) have a greater than average chance of developing diabetes themselves.

Diabetes affects all the peoples of the earth, with
one exception: diabetes is extremely rare among Eski-
mos. The Pima and Papago Indians of the southwest-
ern United States have the highest diabetes rate of
all—72 percent. Scientists point to such statistics as
evidence for a hereditary susceptibility to diabetes,
but some studies make it clear that heredity is not the
whole story. The Yemenite Jews, for example, had

an extremely low diabetes rate before they emigrated to Israel, but after years of living in their new homeland, their diabetes rate rose above that of the Israelis who had originally come from Europe. The explanation for the change is apparently one of life-style, and especially of diet. Yemenites in Israel eat a much richer diet than they used to, and use a great deal of table sugar, which was not a part of their diet before.

In general, any diet (even a vegetarian diet) that results in a gain in weight will increase one's chances of developing diabetes. A diet that causes weight reduction will decrease one's chance of developing diabetes, or, if it is already present, will make it less severe. At least three-quarters of the people who develop diabetes in middle or old age are overweight. Yet not all—or even most—overweight people develop diabetes.

What causes diabetes? Why can't a diabetic's body handle the sugars it needs to provide energy? What other effects does the disease produce? Before examining what goes wrong in the diabetic's body, we need to know something about how the healthy body works.

Stoking the Body's Engines

Your body is a miniature chemical factory. While you sit reading this book, countless numbers of tiny production lines are busily turning out the chemicals you need to breathe, read, turn the page, and think. Thousands of chemical reactions go on constantly, sending messages along nerves, moving muscles, building up body tissues and tearing them down. Similar reactions are going on in every living human.

Like any factory, the human body needs fuel and raw materials. The foods we eat provide a continual supply of these materials. Some are used to build up new body structures. A great deal of building goes on during childhood, when a person is growing actively. But even after growth has stopped, chemical reactions must still go on, to repair and replace damaged or worn-out body parts, and to make the body's machinery work. All these body activities require energy to make them go. Some of the foods we eat are used in the body as fuel. They are chemically combined with oxygen, just as the wood in a bonfire combines with oxygen as it burns. But the oxidation reactions in the body are much more controlled than those of a fire. The energy released is not wasted in heat and light, but instead is mostly stored away in convenient "packets," in the form of chemical bonds contained in a substance called ATP (adenosine triphosphate).

A very few of the substances contained in foods can be used in the body just as they are. But most must first be broken down into simpler substances by the reactions of digestion. Starches, such as those found in potatoes and bread, are digested into sugars, which can pass easily through the walls of the digestive tract into the bloodstream, and then into the body cells. (Both starches and sugars belong to the group of foodstuffs called carbohydrates.) Proteins, which are the main ingredients in meat and fish, are digested into smaller units called amino acids. Fats and oils are broken down into their component parts, called fatty acids and glycerol.

All three types of foodstuffs—carbohydrates, proteins, and fats—can be used as fuel by the body. But if there is enough sugar available, the body will generally use that as fuel in preference to proteins and fats, which have other uses. Proteins are used as the main building materials of the body; they form the bulk of the muscles and skin. Fats are very important parts of the brain, nerves, and other tissues. (Fats, however, can cause trouble if they are deposited inside the linings of the blood vessels. Such fatty deposits cause "hardening of the arteries," which can lead to heart disease and strokes.)

Generally the body uses what food it needs and

stores any extra away. Extra sugars are stored in the liver and muscles in the form of a starch called glycogen. Extra fats are laid down in a number of "fat depots" in various parts of the body—for example, the belly and buttocks. Extra proteins may be changed into sugars or fats for storage, or may be broken down and sent out of the body in the urine. If the food you eat does not contain enough carbohydrates, proteins, and fats to support all the body's activities, the body will live off its reserves, drawing out sugar from the glycogen in the liver and muscles, then taking fat from the fat depots, and, if necessary, even pulling proteins out of the muscles. If you eat more food than you need, the excess will be stored away, mostly as fat in the fat depots. That is why continually eating more food than you need will make you get fat. These days, more and more Americans are doing just that, and obesity is one of our most widespread and serious health problems.

Scientists call the sum total of all the chemical reactions that go on in the body *metabolism*. The reactions that build up new chemicals and structures are referred to as *anabolism*, while those that break down chemicals (such as digestion and oxidation reactions) are called *catabolism*. In a growing child, there are more anabolic reactions going on than catabolic reactions. In an adult, the anabolic and catabolic reactions are generally fairly well balanced. But when a person is sick, there may be more catabolic reactions, and the person may waste away.

Chemicals called *hormones* act on each other and on the cells of the body in very finely tuned harmony to control the body's metabolism. Hormones are produced by the body's endocrine glands, which send their secretions directly into the bloodstream. Blood carries the hormones far and wide, so that secretions of the pituitary gland, nestled up in the brain, may produce their effects even at the tips of the fingers and toes. The pituitary gland and a part of the brain called the hypothalamus act as the master coordinators of the hormone system, controlling the secretions of other endocrine glands. An endocrine gland found in the neck, the thyroid, keeps a close rein on the rate of metabolism. Other endocrine glands produce hormones that control and coordinate other activities of the body.

The gland that is most concerned in the way the body handles sugar is the pancreas. It is a rather curious gland. It's somewhat fish-shaped and lies across the middle of the abdomen, nestled behind the stomach and liver. The odd thing about it is that it is two separate glands in one. Most of the pancreas is not an endocrine gland at all. It produces digestive juices that empty into the intestine through ducts and help us to digest our food. Scattered through the pancreas are small masses of tissue that look quite different from the rest of the tissue in the pancreas when they are viewed under a microscope. These small "islands" dotted throughout the pancreas are the endocrine portion of the gland. They are called the *islets of*

Langerhans after the medical researcher who first described and studied them. The islets themselves contain at least two different kinds of hormone-producing cells, alpha cells and beta cells, and they produce two different hormones. *Insulin*, the hormone of the beta cells, has been the headline-grabber for many years, and most people do not realize that it is not the only hormone secreted by the pancreas. The hormone produced by the alpha cells is called *glucagon*, and scientists are just now coming to realize how important it is.

Although insulin and glucagon are both produced in the pancreas, and both work to control the body's use of sugar (which scientists call sugar metabolism), their effects are almost exactly opposite. Insulin is secreted as a reaction to a rise in the amount of sugar in the blood, and it works to lower the blood sugar level. It does this in a number of ways. Insulin makes it easier for the simple sugar glucose to pass into the body cells. It helps some cells, such as those of the liver, to change glucose into the starch glycogen and put it away in storage. Other cells are prompted by insulin to change glucose into fatty acids, which are also stored away. Insulin also helps the cells to build amino acids into proteins, and keeps them from converting amino acids and fatty acids into sugars.

Glucagon is secreted when the blood sugar level falls, and it works to put more sugar into the blood. Glucagon makes liver cells break down some of their stored glycogen into sugar. It also gives a helping push to the reactions that convert amino acids and fatty acids into glucose. Thus, glucagon and insulin work like two people sitting on opposite ends of a seesaw. If the blood sugar level goes up too high, the amount of insulin rises and pushes the blood sugar down. If the blood sugar level falls too low, glucagon boosts it back up again. Together, the two hormones keep the amount of glucose in the blood moving up and down within a narrow range.

What is the "right amount" of glucose in the blood? In fact, what is the sugar doing in the blood in the first place, and why does the body need a complicated system of hormones to keep it in balance?

Glucose is the favored energy fuel for most cells of the body. (The brain, in particular, needs a steady supply of this vital sugar. Without glucose for energy, the brain can't work properly. If your brain were being "starved," you wouldn't be able to think straight, or move; after a while, you wouldn't even be able to breathe.) Glucose for the hungry cells is carried through the body by the blood. Every beat of the heart pumps blood through the thousands of miles of tiny blood vessels that make up the circulatory system.

A relatively small amount of sugar can supply the needs of the trillions of cells in the human body. All the blood of an average-sized adult man usually contains just about a teaspoon of glucose. But a person's blood sugar level is not the same all the time. It goes up shortly after a meal, when foods from the digestive tract are passing into the bloodstream; and it goes down when a person hasn't eaten for a long time. During your long night's sleep, you don't eat anything, so your blood sugar level is generally lowest just before breakfast. (Your lowest blood sugar level is called your "fasting blood glucose.")

In a healthy person, the swings in blood sugar level are not permitted to go very far. When sugar floods into the blood after a meal, the pancreas quickly secretes insulin, which helps the body cells get the sugar tucked away into storage. When a person has fasted or is starved, glucagon keeps the blood sugar level from falling so low that the body's needs for sugar can't be met. In a healthy person, the blood sugar level rarely rises above a concentration of 160 milligrams in each 100 milliliters of blood (or 160 mg%), even after a meal, or falls below 60 mg%, even during a fast. The average fasting blood sugar level is about 80 mg%.

That is the way the body is *supposed* to work. But what happens in diabetes?

What Goes Wrong?

In a healthy person, the pancreas works like a computer, sending out just enough of the right hormone to keep the blood glucose level within the narrow range of "just enough." But in a diabetic, something has gone wrong with this finely tuned system. The blood sugar rises far above the normal limit—perhaps up to 200, 300, or even 400 mg% or more.

It used to be thought that the reason for this was quite simple: that something happened to damage the beta cells of the pancreas, so that they could not secrete enough insulin to keep the blood sugar level in check. That is the case for *some* diabetics. But as medical researchers have studied diabetes, they have discovered that damage to the beta cells and too little insulin are only part of the puzzle. Some people with very serious cases of diabetes have beta cells that look perfectly normal. Tests of their blood show that there is plenty of insulin there—more than enough, it would seem, to keep their sugar metabolism running smoothly. Yet they too suffer from *hyperglycemia* (too much sugar in the blood).

Diabetes specialists now believe that a diabetic condition may arise in a number of ways. Damage to the beta cells, so that the pancreas cannot produce enough insulin, is one of them. High blood sugar could also result if the pancreas is producing normal amounts of insulin, but the body's needs for the hormone become far higher than normal and the gland cannot keep up. This might happen when people overeat to an extreme degree, flooding their bodies with more carbohydrates than their systems can handle. Or, if the thyroid gland goes out of order and becomes too active, it can increase the rate at which insulin is used up so that a relative insulin shortage results.

In some cases of diabetes, the insulin that the pancreas produces does not work properly. This may happen for one of several reasons. For example, the body normally produces a chemical called insulinase, which breaks down excess insulin when its job is done. If too much insulinase is produced, the insulin will be destroyed before it has had a chance to lower the body's blood sugar level. Sometimes the body produces antibodies against insulin, in much the same way it produces antibodies against disease germs. Normally this shouldn't happen—antibodies are a body defense against "foreign invaders"; but the body sometimes makes mistakes, and its defenders may fail to recognize its own chemicals. Antibodies or other chemicals produced in the body may attack insulin or attach themselves to its molecules so that the insulin cannot work on the cells. Damage to the beta cells might cause them to produce a faulty kind of insulin that is not as effective as the normal kind. Certain drugs, including cortisone, nicotinic acid, and some diuretics (drugs that are used to rid the body of excess fluids), can interfere with the action of insulin.

Diabetes may also result from too much glucagon, rather than not enough insulin. Many diabetics are found to have higher-than-normal levels of glucagon in their blood. Recently, researchers have discovered a new hormone, *somatostatin*, that helps to regulate the secretion of the hormones of the pancreas. Curiously, injections of somatostatin decrease the secretion of both glucagon and insulin—but they improve the blood sugar levels of diabetics because they have a greater effect in reducing the secretion of glucagon, the blood sugar–raising hormone. Somatostatin is secreted mainly by the hypothalamus, which is in the brain, but it is also produced in other organs of the body, including the delta cells of the pancreas.

Some of the latest studies of diabetes have been focused on the last link in the chain of insulin activity: the interaction between insulin and the cell. The pancreas may be normal and may produce perfectly good insulin on cue whenever the blood sugar level rises—yet the insulin may not be able to do its work if there is something wrong with the outer surface of the cells. Researchers have found that insulin normally reacts with specific chemicals, called receptors, on the cells' outer membranes. If there are not enough of these receptors, or if they are not the right kind to react with insulin, the hormone will not be able to help the cells lower the body's blood sugar level.

Describing *how* diabetes may develop is not the same thing as explaining *why* it happens. Just as a diabetic condition may be the result of any one of several things, it is believed that diabetes has not one single cause, but, rather, many causes. Some of these are still unknown, but researchers have already discovered a number of clues. And some of the newest findings have turned many old ideas about the condition upside down.

If you read a book about diabetes that was written before about 1976 or so, you may find a statement like, "Diabetes is not contagious. You can't 'catch' diabetes." That is still true in one respect: you don't need to fear that you will come down with diabetes if you work or play with a diabetic, or if you live with a diabetic parent, child, or spouse. Yet a number of recent studies have suggested that at least one type of diabetes *is* in fact infectious. However, you can't catch it in quite the same way you would catch a cold or flu or tuberculosis—it's much more complicated than that.

Medical workers have noticed that diabetes in children, normally a rather rare disease (though it is growing ever more common), tends to occur in clusters. A number of cases will suddenly crop up in a particular locality. Careful studies of health records have shown that outbreaks of juvenile diabetes often follow an epidemic of a virus disease, such as mumps or rubella (German measles). A group of viruses called Coxsackie viruses have also been implicated. In some cases, the diabetes "epidemic" follows the virus epidemic closely; in others, there seems to be a period of about three or four years between the outbreak of the virus disease and the appearance of symptoms of diabetes.

Of course, it may be that the extra stress of the virus disease is just too much for a person who happens to have a weak pancreas, and the gland breaks down when the body is under siege by the disease germs. But researchers wonder whether the virus might actually cause damage to the pancreas, in addition to having its more obvious effects. They think this might occur in two ways. Viruses might actually invade the pancreas and destroy the beta cells. Or the virus particles might happen to be a bit similar, chemically, to part of the surface of the beta cells. Then antibodies produced by the body to attack the viruses would also attack and destroy beta cells.

There is a good deal of evidence to support such views. Juvenile diabetics usually make little or no insulin, and examinations of tissue from their pancreases show that beta cells have indeed been destroyed. Often antibodies against these cells can be found circulating in a juvenile diabetic's blood. And studies of animals have revealed that some viruses actually do make a beeline for the pancreas, where they attack and destroy beta cells; such animals develop a condition that is very similar to juvenile diabetes in humans.

Most researchers now believe that many cases of

juvenile diabetes are probably caused by virus infections. It may take several years for viruses lurking in
the body to do enough damage to the pancreas to
produce actual symptoms of diabetes. (The viruses
are thus like a fire that smolders unnoticed in a pile of
trash for a long time before it suddenly bursts into
flames.) Or the diabetic condition may be the result
of a series of virus infections, each of which does its
own bit of damage to the beta cells until insulin
production is no longer able to meet the body's needs.

All children catch virus diseases—usually a number
of them during the growing years. Yet most children
don't develop diabetes. Why? What determines that a
virus infection will cause diabetes in one child, while
another child will suffer the same infection and re-
cover with full health? If juvenile diabetes is indeed
an *autoimmune* disease—one in which the body makes
antibodies against a virus that also attack its own
body cells—then a child who does *not* develop diabetes after a virus infection may just have been lucky
enough not to produce those destructive antibodies. It
is known that each person produces his or her own
unique antibodies against any particular germ or
chemical. One person's antibodies might be quite different from those of other people, yet do the same
job. So some children may produce antibodies that
just cure them of the viral infection without affecting
the pancreas.

Another possibility is that a person may inherit a
pancreas that is particularly susceptible to virus at-

tack. Recent studies have shown that most juvenile diabetics have several specific types of chemicals on the surface of their cells that are not usually found in other people. These cell-surface chemicals, which are hereditary, might be the key to the increased vulnerability of the pancreas. They might be the chemicals against which a person's body makes antibodies when viruses attack. Or they might serve as chemical "hooks" by which invading viruses can attach themselves to the beta cells. (Interestingly, maturity-onset diabetics do not show the same sort of correlation with special cell-surface chemicals that juvenile diabetics do.)

Before the role of viruses in juvenile diabetes was suspected, it was thought that this was a hereditary disease—that two "bad" genes, one carried by each parent, could combine in the child to produce the disease. Thus two seemingly normal, nondiabetic parents could have diabetic children. If one of the parents was a diabetic, the chances of a child's inheriting the disease would be even greater. But genetic studies have indicated that things don't work that way after all. Studies of identical twins have been especially enlightening. Identical twins share exactly the same heredity. So if juvenile diabetes is inherited, you would expect that if one twin has juvenile diabetes, the other will have it too. Researchers were surprised to find that this was not the case. Dr. Priscilla White and other scientists at the Joslin Diabetes Foundation in Boston surveyed groups of juvenile diabetics who had identical twins and found that only about half the other twins also had the disease. Even 50 percent, of course, is much higher than the probability of two unrelated persons' having diabetes. But the fact that half the time both twins did have juvenile diabetes is not necessarily an indication that the disease is hereditary, because twins, living together, would be likely to catch the same virus diseases—either from their friends or from each other.

Quite a different result was found when the researchers studied identical twins who developed diabetes at the age of forty or later. If one of those twins was diabetic, then 90 percent of the time the other was too. So it seems that heredity may indeed be involved in cases of diabetes appearing in middle and old age.

Researchers now believe that the heredity of diabetes is rather complicated—that there is not a single "diabetes gene," but that a number of genes are involved, and that they interact with one another and can be affected by many things.

One of the most important factors in the development of diabetes in adults seems to be overweight. The rich diet most Americans eat and the lazy habits most of us have developed now that automobiles and office jobs are so common are turning us into a nation of fat people. Most people who develop diabetes in middle or old age are overweight when the disease develops. Often, if they manage to bring their weight down by strict dieting and exercise, the symptoms of the disease disappear.

There are good reasons for this. First of all, people generally get overweight by overeating—taking in more food than the body needs to fuel its activities. Much of this extra food is carbohydrate. Cake, cookies, potato chips, candy, soft drinks, and other favorites add to the sugar in our diet. The rise in blood glucose after each heavy meal stimulates the secretion of insulin. As we get older, body cells wear out, and the body's systems for repairing and replacing worn-out cells grow less effective. The pancreas is no exception. If we continue to overload our beta cells for years by overeating, they may grow too old and tired to respond to the body's call for insulin.

In addition, researchers have found that the body's need for insulin rises when a person is overweight. Even a normal pancreas may not be able to keep up with the demands imposed by extra pounds of weight. For example, if the pancreas is capable of turning out a normal amount of insulin, but the body needs twice the normal amount because it is twice the size it should be, then there will not be enough insulin to meet the body's need, and sugar will build up in the blood.

Even if the pancreas of an obese person is able to produce the increased amounts of insulin the person needs, problems may develop. For as extra insulin circulates in the blood, body cells begin to tear down some of their surface insulin receptors. This is a protective reaction, one by which the cells try to keep their metabolism in balance. If there is a great deal of insulin in the blood, a decrease in the number of receptors makes the cells less sensitive to the hormone and keeps them from being overwhelmed by its effects. (Cells can also *increase* the number of receptors on their surface membranes if insulin levels fall. Thus, they can become more sensitive to insulin and compensate for a failing pancreas—for a while.) As the number of insulin receptors decreases, the circulating insulin becomes less effective, and a rising blood sugar level signals the pancreas to produce even more insulin—which in turn stimulates a further decrease in cellular insulin receptors. Eventually the overworked beta cells may simply give up!

What happens to the body when the blood sugar level rises? For one thing, the kidneys are affected. All the blood in the body is continually filtered through these two large, bean-shaped organs. The kidneys get rid of many of the body's waste products and poisons, along with enough water to flush them out of the body. Blood cells and large molecules such as proteins are held back by the kidneys' filters. As the forming urine trickles through the kidneys, there is a continual trading of chemicals back and forth. If there is too much of something in the blood—a particular salt, for example—the excess passes into the urine. If there is just enough of a substance, or even a shortage of it, the kidneys will hold it back, and it will pass back into the blood. In a healthy person, there is just the right amount of glucose in the blood, so the kidneys hold it all back. Normally there is no sugar in the urine. But when the blood sugar level rises beyond about 180 mg%, the excess sugar begins to "spill" over into the urine. (Remember that the highest the blood sugar normally goes is about 160 mg%.) The presence of glucose in the urine is called *glucosuria*.

The kidneys are used to producing urine of a particular concentration. This may vary somewhat during the day—you've probably noticed that your urine looks and smells much "stronger" first thing in the morning, when it has been accumulating all night, than it does later in the day. But there must always be enough water in the urine to keep irritating and poisonous nitrogen wastes well diluted. As the amount of glucose spilling into a diabetic's urine increases, the urine becomes more concentrated. So the kidneys must put out more water to keep the urine diluted enough. When they do this, the body becomes dehydrated, and the person becomes thirsty.

With all the extra water flowing out through the kidneys, extra minerals are washed out too; even proteins and fats, which are not normally excreted by the kidneys, may be washed out. Vitamins are also lost. Losing all this sugar and water, and all these vitamins, minerals, proteins, and fats, the uncontrolled diabetic begins to lose weight. A sudden weight loss after a long period of gaining weight is one of the danger signals that can point to unsuspected diabetes.

Meanwhile, despite all that sugar floating around in the blood, the diabetic is unable to use sugar effectively as a fuel for normal body activities. Chemical distress signals are sent out by the hungry cells, and a metabolic switch-over begins. The body begins to raid its fat stores for energy fuel, and it may even begin to pull protein from the muscles. (That's like a family who have run out of fuel oil chopping up their furniture and burning it in the fireplace to keep warm—it may solve the problem temporarily, but it creates even worse problems later.)

When fats are broken down for energy (a process that does not involve insulin), chemicals called *ketone bodies* are formed as by-products. These build up in the blood and spill over into the urine; they may give the breath of a diabetic a distinctive "fruity," acetone odor. Ketone bodies are somewhat acid, and they upset the acid balance of the blood. This is a delicate balance, and it is normally maintained within very close limits. Too much acid can poison or even kill the body cells. If too much fat must be used to provide energy because there is not enough insulin to allow the use of glucose for fuel, a state called *ketoacidosis* develops. A person who develops ketoacidosis may lose consciousness, may go into a coma, and—if not rescued by prompt medical treatment—may die.

Today most diabetics do not die of diabetic coma. But if a diabetic's condition is not well controlled, prolonged periods of high blood sugar can lead to very serious complications. About half the diabetics who develop the disease in childhood eventually die of kidney failure. Dialysis, a process by which special filters remove poisons and waste products from the blood when the kidneys can no longer do it, has brought new hope to diabetics suffering from this complication of their disease. So have kidney transplants; yet unless a diabetic's condition is controlled, high blood sugar levels will eventually damage the new kidney too.

Diabetics are two to five times as likely as non-diabetics to die of heart disease or a stroke. There are a number of reasons for this increased risk. Diabetics are particularly likely to develop high blood pressure, which forces the heart to work harder and may lead to a stroke. (Recent studies have also linked a high-sugar diet with the development of high blood pressure.) Diabetics are also very prone to develop *arteriosclerosis*, or hardening of the arteries. In this condition, fat deposits form in the linings of the arteries. Salts are added to these growing deposits, and eventually they may close the artery completely. Or they may narrow the artery so much that a blood clot plugs it, cutting off the flow of blood "downstream." If the artery happens to serve a key organ of the body, such as the heart or brain, a heart attack or stroke can result.

There has been some argument in medical circles about whether diabetes actually causes arteriosclerosis or merely brings on aging of the circulatory system earlier than usual. Doctors have also debated whether better control of blood sugar levels can really help to prevent this serious complication. The current view is that high sugar concentrations in the blood *do* contribute to hardening of the arteries, but researchers are not yet sure how they produce that effect.

Diabetics are more susceptible to infections than nondiabetics, and infected cuts and sores may be very slow to heal. There are a number of reasons for this. High-sugar blood provides rich nourishment for invading microbes. The poor circulation that a diabetic may develop hampers the delivery of the chemicals and nutrients that are needed for healing and repair of injuries. A lack of insulin interferes with repair processes, since, like other body activities, repair processes require the use of sugar for energy. The immune system, a main defense against foreign invaders, does not seem to work as well in diabetics; in particular, the white blood cells, which normally act as roving defenders for the body, are impaired.

Progressive nerve damage may make a diabetic gradually lose his or her sense of touch, and may produce tormenting pains in the arms and legs. Researchers now believe that these complications are caused by a conversion of some of the excess glucose in the blood to another sugar, *sorbitol*, which is deposited in the nerves. As sorbitol builds up, the nerves lose a chemical, *myoinositol*, that they need to function.

Sorbitol is also thought to be the culprit in one of the eye problems that often plague diabetics. When the blood sugar level is high, sorbitol builds up in the eyes, which are actually fluid-filled balls. As the sorbitol concentration increases, the fluid in the eyes gets thicker, and water flows in from surrounding tissues to dilute the fluid. Fluctuations in the blood sugar level during the day may cause the eyeballs to swell as they fill with extra fluid (when the sugar level is high), and then contract (as the sugar level drops). Since the size and shape of the eyeballs determine how images are focused on the retina, the diabetic's vision may be blurred, and he or she may become temporarily nearsighted or farsighted. As long as the blood sugar level is seesawing back and forth this way, the vision problems can't even be corrected with glasses, for the prescription may change from hour to hour. Even after treatment of diabetes has begun, getting a prescription for eyeglasses may have to be postponed for some weeks, until the blood sugar level is well under control and the refraction of the eyes has stabilized.

In long-standing diabetes, a more serious visual problem known as *diabetic retinopathy* may develop. Tiny blood vessels grow out across the eye and begin to bleed, blocking part of the vision. Eventually cataracts may form, and these can result in blindness. In fact, diabetes is the leading cause of blindness in the United States.

The effects of diabetes and its complications form a distressing catalog of symptoms and disabilities. Fortunately, there are a number of effective ways of diagnosing diabetes early, and treatments that can help to prevent its disabling and life-threatening effects in many patients. Our knowledge of diabetes and our arsenal of weapons for fighting it are the fruits of many centuries of study, but the greatest successes have come within the last few generations.

A Look Backward

When did diabetes begin? Did the prehistoric cave dwellers suffer from it? We have no way of being sure. But from what has been observed and reported about this condition in historic times, we might suspect that it was not very common among the earliest humans. Before farming and herding were developed, people probably scratched out a rather bare existence, getting plenty of exercise and rarely having a chance to eat more food than they needed. Seldom did they live long enough to develop the diseases of middle and old age. It is likely that diabetes did not come to play an important role in human health until people began to accumulate wealth and leisure, and could choose to lead "the good life."

The first recorded mention of diabetes is in an Egyptian manuscript called the Ebers papyrus, which was written in about 1500 B.C. The physicians of ancient Egypt had a great deal of knowledge and skill, and the Ebers papyrus and others from a few centuries later provide prescriptions for relieving *polyuria*, or frequent urination.

The ancient Greeks were also familiar with diabetes. The Greek physician Aretaeus of Cappadocia

46 /

gave the disease its name. About 100 A.D. he wrote a description of his observations:

> Diabetes is a wonderful affliction, not very frequent among men, being a melting down of the flesh and limbs into urine. The patients never stop making water . . . the flow is incessant, as if opening an aqueduct. Life is short, disgusting, and painful; thirst unquenchable; excessive drinking . . . is disproportionate to the large quantity of urine, for more urine is passed; and one cannot stop them either from drinking or making water. Or if for a time they abstain from drinking, their mouth becomes parched and their body dry; the viscera seem as if scorched up; they are affected with nausea, restlessness, and burning thirst; and at no distant term they expire.

Aretaeus' prescription for this affliction was a diet of milk, gruel, cereal, and wine.

Diabetes was also well known to medical specialists in ancient Asia. Sushrutha, a physician in India, described "honey urine" back in 400 B.C., and noted that the urine of diabetics attracts flies. Other ancient Indian writers described such symptoms as thirst, fatigue, and skin boils. They reported that diabetes is a disease most often found among the rich and self-indulgent, who are fond of eating to excess; they also suggested that the disease might be hereditary. But they had no cures to offer. Chinese and Japanese doctors of this period also described cases of polyuria in which the urine had a sweet taste and attracted dogs, and noted that the disease was often accompanied by skin boils.

In the West, Roman physicians picked up the study of diabetes where the Greeks had left off. But then came the Dark Ages, when much of the old knowledge was lost and little new progress in medicine was made.

The Renaissance brought a rebirth of interest in all the mysteries of our world, including the workings of the human body. Paracelsus, a Swiss physician who lived in the fifteenth century, almost made a great discovery about diabetes. He evaporated the urine of a diabetic and found that a white powder remained when all the liquid was gone. But he mistakenly thought this powder was salt, and concluded that salt is the cause of the diabetic's frequent urination.

Other European physicians tried tasting the urine of diabetics and decided that it contained sugar. The English physician Thomas Sydenham, who lived in the 1600s, tried a meat diet (high in protein) for his diabetic patients and found that they improved; the sugar in their urine often disappeared.

In 1683, Swiss researcher Johann Conrad Brunner tried an experiment on dogs. He removed their pancreases and kept the dogs alive. He noticed that they suffered from great thirst and excessive urination, but he did not realize that he had created an experimental model of diabetes. No one else realized the significance of his findings either, and his observations were mostly unnoticed.

In the years that followed, scientists learned more about chemistry, and in 1766 Matthew Dobson was able to establish definitely that the sweetness of diabetic urine was due to the presence of sugar. In 1783 English physician Thomas Cawley was the first to record a diagnosis of diabetes mellitus on the basis of sugar in the urine.

For a time, physicians had to taste their patients' urine to determine whether sugar was present, but in the early nineteenth century German physician Johann Frank relieved them of this unpleasant task by inventing a yeast test for sugar. Around this time, doctors such as the British physician John Rollo were experimenting with low-carbohydrate diets in the treatment of diabetes, and during the 1800s a high fat intake, green vegetables, and exercise were typically prescribed. Such treatments sometimes helped diabetics get better—especially if they were obese older people. But juvenile diabetics were doomed. Once their disease developed, there was little doctors could do for them, and they usually had only a few months to live.

Until the late 1800s, doctors were able to treat some of the symptoms of diabetes, but they had no clear idea of what was causing the symptoms. Back in 1788, Thomas Cawley almost made a key discovery. While doing an autopsy of a diabetic patient, he noticed that the pancreas didn't look quite normal. But he never followed up this observation, because he was convinced that diabetes was a disease of the kidneys.

The first big breakthrough came in 1889, and it came by accident. In Europe, medical researchers J. von Mering and O. Minkowski were studying the digestion of fats. They thought the pancreas might be involved in this (we know now that it is). So they removed the pancreas of a dog to see what would happen. The dog survived the operation, but then it began to urinate copiously, as Brunner's dogs had over two hundred years earlier, and clouds of flies gathered around the puddles of urine. Their supervisor, Bernhard Naunyn, noticed what was happening, and suggested they analyze the dog's urine. Sure enough, it contained sugar; the dog had developed a classic case of diabetes mellitus. Von Mering and Minkowski recognized the significance of their findings, and repeated the experiment on other dogs. Each time, removal of the pancreas produced all the symptoms of diabetes mellitus. So diabetes was a disease of the pancreas, not the kidneys. But what could a digestive gland like the pancreas have to do with diabetes?

Another piece of the puzzle was already in place, waiting to be recognized. In 1869 a brilliant German medical student, Paul Langerhans, had noticed the clusters of cells now called the islets of Langerhans scattered through the pancreas. Other researchers followed up his work and discovered that the islets have nothing to do with the digestive functions of the pancreas but are, rather, endocrine glands. Autopsies of diabetics, performed in 1902 at Johns Hopkins Uni-

versity in Baltimore, revealed that the islets of
Langerhans had degenerated. Laboratory studies
helped to confirm the link between the islets and diabetes. In experiments on animals, conducted in several laboratories, the ducts of the pancreas were tied
off; the gland shriveled, but the islets of Langerhans
remained undamaged, and no symptoms of diabetes
appeared. But if the whole pancreas was removed, or
if the islets were damaged, diabetes developed.

Meanwhile, two different types of islet cells, alpha
and beta cells, were identified, and scientists
theorized that each produced a hormone. In the early
1900s, several researchers suggested that one of the
pancreatic hormones controlled sugar metabolism, and proposed that it be called "insulin." But efforts to isolate the hormone were frustrating, and
extracts of the pancreas proved quite ineffective in
treating diabetics.

Now the stage was set for a great medical
breakthrough. Researchers knew the pancreas made
a hormone that was active in sugar metabolism, and
they were eager to isolate it, for it would make an ex-
cellent treatment for diabetes. It seemed only a matter of time before one of the great endocrinologists
would overcome the technical difficulties and isolate
the hormone. But as it turned out, the men who accomplished this feat were not among the big names in
the field; at the time, they could be regarded almost
as amateurs.

When World War I ended, a young Canadian military surgeon named Frederick Banting was mustered out and began a private practice as an orthopedic surgeon in London, Ontario. Business was slow for a young surgeon just starting out on his own. Banting waited a whole month before he had his first patient, and treating this person netted him the grand sum of four dollars. Sitting in the office all day waiting for patients, Dr. Banting had plenty of spare time, and he amused himself by reading medical journals. He became interested in articles about diabetes, because a neighbor's child had recently died of this disease. Reading about the experiments in which the ducts of the pancreas were tied off, Banting got an idea for a new experiment. The reason that extracts of the pancreas had not yielded an active hormone, he theorized, was that the powerful digestive enzymes of the pancreas must be digesting the hormone of the islets during the extraction process. If the ducts were first tied off, the digestive portion of the pancreas would shrivel and stop producing its digestive juices. Then the hormone could be extracted without being destroyed in the process.

To test his idea, Banting needed a laboratory. He went to the Chief of Biochemistry at the University of Toronto, Professor John J. R. Macleod, to ask for support. Macleod refused, because the university was just in the process of building a new medical school, and funds and lab space were scarce. Banting, however, was a persuasive talker, and finally he got permission to run an experiment on ten dogs for a period of eight weeks. Macleod assigned a young graduate student, Charles Best, to the project, and then went off on his summer vacation.

Best was enthusiastic about the project. He was the son of a doctor, and his aunt had died in diabetic coma. The two young researchers roamed the streets of Toronto, hunting for stray dogs, and Banting sold his car to get money for the experiment.

Banting and Best tied off the pancreatic ducts of several experimental dogs; then, after several weeks, they removed the dogs' pancreases. They froze the organs in brine, chopped them up in a mortar, and then injected the salt solution into the veins of normal dogs. The dogs' blood sugar levels fell! Next the researchers injected the extract into dogs previously made diabetic by removal of their pancreases. Their blood sugar levels fell too! In fact, if enough of the extract was injected, the blood sugar level fell below normal.

Banting and Best wanted to call their hormone extract "isletin," but Professor Macleod, back from his vacation, insisted that the older name insulin be used.

Excitement spread through the lab, and the experiments continued. Banting and Best tried their insulin injections on human patients at Toronto General Hospital in 1921. The first patient ever to receive insulin was an eleven-year-old boy named Leonard Thompson. His diabetes had been diagnosed two years before, and doctors had used the only treatment they knew of—a starvation diet of only four hundred fifty calories a day. The boy was still alive, but just barely; he weighed only seventy-five pounds. The insulin injections brought his blood sugar level down dramatically. He was able to eat a more normal diet, gained weight, and lived to maturity.

The next patient was a physician himself. Joseph Gilchrist had just been diagnosed as a diabetic, and he eagerly offered himself as a "human guinea pig." Each new sample of insulin was tested on him. Some injections caused Gilchrist's blood sugar to fall sharply to very low levels. This condition of *hypoglycemia* (low blood sugar) produced mental confusion, weakness, and even unconsciousness. Gilchrist gave the researchers careful medical descriptions of all the symptoms of his reactions to insulin overdoses, and provided the first account in medical history of the condition known as *insulin shock*.

Banting presented a paper on his discovery at the 1921 meeting of the Association of American Physicians, and interest in his work grew. Professor Macleod assigned his whole staff to work on the problems of isolating insulin and running experiments on it. At first it took half a pound of pancreas from a steer to produce enough insulin to treat one patient for two weeks. But Best developed methods for large-scale production. Soon commercial manufacturers were producing supplies of the hormone for doctors to use on diabetic patients all around the world.

In 1923 the Nobel Prize in medicine and physiology was awarded to Frederick Banting and John Macleod for the work on insulin. Banting was furious. It had been his idea, and he and Charles Best had done all the work on the basic discovery, yet Best was not even mentioned in the award. At first Banting refused to accept the prize, but eventually he did, and he immediately gave half of his twenty-five-thousand-dollar share of the award to Charles Best. Macleod also gave away half of his share of the money—to Professor J. B. Collip, who had purified the insulin for the clinical tests.

The insulin breakthrough marked a turning point in the treatment of diabetes. Before insulin was isolated, the only approach that was even partially successful was a severely restricted diet. One such diet was devised by F. M. Allen in 1914. The Allen diet contained very few calories and emphasized vegetables cooked in three changes of water, bran, and olive oil. This diet saved many lives, but patients following it had a miserable existence. One twelve-year-old boy grew so desperate that he ate his toothpaste and his pet canary's birdseed. And even this near-starvation diet prolonged the lives of juvenile diabetics for only a few years. Insulin changed the picture dramatically. With it, juvenile diabetics could hope to grow to adulthood, and all diabetics could eat enough food so that they no longer looked like living skeletons.

For a while after Banting's and Best's discovery, research on diabetes stood still. In the excitement of the insulin breakthrough, people assumed that the diabetes problem was licked, and needed no further attention. The hormone of the alpha cells, glucagon, was discovered two years after Banting and Best isolated insulin, but then it was largely ignored for five decades. Research efforts were concentrated mainly on developing purer and more effective variations of insulin, including long-acting forms whose blood sugar–lowering effects would last for twenty-four hours or more. Scientists dreamed wistfully of inventing an insulin that could be swallowed instead of injected, but they knew this was a hopeless quest: if insulin, a protein, were taken into the stomach, it would quickly be digested to its amino acid constituents, which would be no good at all in treating diabetes.

Slowly, however, dissatisfaction grew. Insulin does not help *all* diabetics. Some people are not willing to submit to a routine of injecting themselves every day, or are too old, feeble, or blind to do so. Even when diabetes seems to be under fairly good control, serious complications of the disease may still develop. And a diabetic taking insulin must constantly walk a tightrope between the danger of taking too small a dose and the danger of taking too large a dose. Too small a dose will produce too high a blood sugar level (or hyperglycemia) and perhaps even diabetic coma; too large a dose will result in too low a blood sugar level (or hypoglycemia), which might lead to equally hazardous insulin shock. So gradually researchers began to look again for better ways of treating diabetes—for drugs that would lower the blood sugar level and could be taken by mouth.

Again a key discovery was made by taking advantage of a lucky accident. In 1948 French researchers R. Jonbon and A. L. Loubatières, of the Institute of Biology at Montpellier, were testing sulfa drugs for typhoid fever. One of the compounds they were using produced an unexpected reaction in rats: it lowered their blood sugar levels. Follow-up studies led to a family of oral hypoglycemic drugs called the sulfonylureas. (Hypoglycemic drugs, as you might guess, are drugs that lower the blood sugar level.) Some had too many bad side effects to be usable, but others have found use in the treatment of diabetic patients. There has been a controversy in recent years about how effective and safe the oral hypoglycemic drugs really are, and their future is somewhat in doubt. But the search for new and better oral drugs for diabetes is continuing.

Still another recent chapter in the diabetes story has dealt with efforts to learn more about the chemistry of the disease and the hormones involved in it. Insulin was the first protein whose complete chemical structure was worked out. Frederick Sanger, a brilliant biochemist from Cambridge, England, took ten years to accomplish this feat, which he completed in 1955. Developing some new methods and ingenious variations, he worked out the exact order of all fifty-one amino acids in the insulin molecule and the way they are linked together in two chains; in 1958 he received a Nobel Prize for this accomplishment.

If scientists know the chemical structure of a substance, they can think about the possibility of making it. The idea of manufacturing synthetic insulin is especially attractive. The insulin used to treat diabetics today comes from the pancreases of cattle and hogs, as a by-product of their slaughter for meat. But the supply of livestock is shrinking, and the number of diabetics is growing. At some point there may not be enough insulin to go around. Moreover, some doctors have expressed concern about possible harmful effects from the long-term use of cattle or hog insulin. Unlike many other hormones, which work only in animals of the species that produced them, insulin from a steer or hog seems to work well in humans, producing the same effect as our own, human insulin. But the molecules of insulin from other species, though very similar chemically, are not *exactly* the same as molecules of human insulin. Diabetics taking animal insulin soon begin producing antibodies against it. These antibodies probably make the insulin less effective, and may have other effects that we do not yet know about—perhaps they are even responsible for some of the problems that are now regarded as complications of diabetes. If we had a cheap source of synthetic *human* insulin, it might be much better than the insulins that are now being used.

In the mid-1960s, three separate groups, working independently, announced the synthesis of insulin. These groups were led by Helmut Zahn of West Germany, P. G. Katsoyannis at the University of Pittsburgh, and Y. C. Du of China. The techniques they used are not suitable for mass production, since they are very complicated and expensive. The process involves two hundred thirty-four separate chemical reactions and produces only very small amounts of the final product. However, several approaches to the commercial manufacture of synthetic insulin are now being developed.

Testing for Diabetes

Do you have diabetes? Yes? No? How do you know for sure?

A variety of tests for diabetes are used, for a number of different purposes. There are quick and easy tests suitable for screening large groups of the population. Every time you supply a urine specimen at a routine medical checkup, the doctor or an assistant should give it a quick check for sugar, even if there is no particular reason to suspect that you might be suffering from diabetes. These tests are also used routinely by diabetics to monitor how well their condition is being controlled. Other, more complicated tests provide more information: if diabetes is present, how serious is it, and what kind of diabetes is it? Such tests are used when a doctor already suspects a person of having diabetes; they provide information that helps the doctor plan methods of treatment, and they can also be used to check on how well treatment is working. Some especially sophisticated tests, now being refined, give an idea of whether a person *might* come down with diabetes at some time in the future.

The simplest and most commonly used tests for

diabetes are the urine tests. One type, *Clinitest*, consists of a tablet that is dropped into a test tube containing five drops of urine and ten drops of water. A chemical reaction takes place, and the liquid changes color. A blue color means that no sugar is present. Green indicates a small amount of sugar, about 0.5 percent. Yellow corresponds to about 1 percent sugar, orange to more than 1 percent, and orange-red to more than 2 percent. (Remember that normal urine contains *no* sugar.)

Diastix is a plastic strip with a small treated paper square at one end. The strip is dipped into the urine, and the color of the paper square is noted after 30 seconds. Blue-green is negative (there is no sugar in the blood) and brown positive (sugar is present).

Another commonly used urine test is *Tes-Tape*. Tes-Tape is a roll of yellow paper that comes in a container something like a Scotch tape dispenser. In the presence of sugar, an enzyme in the treated paper reacts and releases a dye. A strip of tape is torn off, dipped in a urine specimen, and then read after about a minute. Tes-Tape stays yellow in the absence of sugar; if it turns blue, that means about 2 percent sugar is present. (Some users get confused, for the colors are the opposite of those with Clinitest and Diastix.)

Of these three tests, Clinitest and Diastix are the most accurate in showing the amounts of sugar present, and Diastix and Tes-Tape are the most convenient to use. The use of certain medications may give a false positive reaction with Clinitest and Tes-Tape, producing the characteristic color change even when no sugar is present. Clinitest is also sensitive to sugars other than glucose, such as lactose, which is present in the urine of a nursing mother. Diastix does not give false positives, but certain drugs may produce a false *negative* reaction.

One advantage of Diastix is that the results will not be affected by the presence of ascorbic acid (vitamin C). These days, many people take vitamin C supplements regularly because they believe this vitamin will help them to avoid colds. (Some researchers have also suggested that large doses of vitamin C may be helpful in treating diabetes.) When large amounts of this vitamin are consumed, the amount the body cannot use is flushed out in the urine, and may distort some of the tests for urinary sugar.

Other simple tests, such as *Ketostix* and *Acetest*, can be used to check for the presence of ketone bodies in the urine—a sign of an uncontrolled diabetic condition.

Diabetics under treatment may be asked by the doctor to test their urine once a day, or even more often. The first urine specimen produced after waking in the morning shows whether any sugar has spilled over during the night. Often the diabetic is asked to discard that specimen and test the next one, produced half an hour or an hour later. That test will show whether any sugar is spilling *now*. Other tests may be made before or after meals.

One problem with using urine tests to screen for new cases of diabetes is that a person's blood sugar level must be fairly high before any glucose will spill over into the urine. Some people's kidneys will tolerate comparatively large amounts of sugar in the blood before passing it into the urine. Other people may have sugar in the urine but perfectly normal blood sugar levels, because their kidneys will tolerate only a small amount of sugar in the blood. Since the diagnosis of diabetes depends on the finding of abnormally high sugar levels in the *blood*, positive urine sugar tests only indicate the *possibility* of the presence of diabetes; they should never be used to definitively diagnose the disease.

A variety of blood tests are used to get information on a person's blood sugar level. These are all more precise than urine tests. The simplest blood test is the test for *fasting glucose* level. For this test, a doctor uses a blood specimen taken in the morning, before the person has eaten anything. Normal values are considered to be between 60 and 110 milligrams of sugar in each 100 milliliters of blood plasma (or 60 to 110 mg%), but the upper normal limit is increased by about 2 mg% for each decade of life after age thirty. Values as high as 140 mg% are sometimes seen in elderly people who do not have diabetes. But in young and middle-aged people, a fasting glucose level above 130 mg% is usually considered an indication of diabetes.

Sometimes, in mild forms of diabetes, the pancreas

can maintain a normal blood sugar level when not much stress is being put on it, but it can't cope with the large influx of sugar that floods into the blood when a person eats a heavy meal or a very rich dessert. For this reason, a test of a blood sample drawn two hours after a meal containing a fair amount of carbohydrate is a more reliable test than the fasting glucose level in diagnosing mild diabetes. Normal blood sugar levels two hours after eating are about 20 mg% higher than fasting glucose.

If there is any doubt about the diagnosis of diabetes, a doctor may order a *glucose tolerance* test. After a blood specimen is taken for determination of the fasting glucose level, the person is given a measured amount of a very concentrated glucose solution to drink. (You might think that would be a tasty treat, but it is just too much sweetness, and most people have to struggle to get it all down.) Then blood specimens are taken again after one, two, and three hours. The glucose levels in each of the four blood samples may be plotted on a graph, and will show a sharp rise as the sugar passes into the blood, and then a fall as insulin brings the blood sugar level down again. The height of the rise and how quickly the sugar level falls show how well the pancreas can cope with a sugar load. Too high a rise or too slow a fall usually is an indication of diabetes.

Certain drugs may interfere with glucose metabolism, so that tests show high blood sugar levels in people who are not diabetic. These drugs include steroid hormones, birth control pills, caffeine (the "drug" found in coffee, tea, and cola drinks), and nicotine (the active ingredient in cigarettes). Very stressful situations, such as a severe infection, a heart attack or stroke, or pregnancy, may also produce impaired glucose tolerance; blood sugar levels usually return to normal after the stress is eased.

A new testing technique called *radioimmunoassay*, developed by Solomon Berson and Rosalyn Yalow (who won a Nobel Prize for her work), has made it possible to test the levels of insulin in the blood. Use of this technique in the 1950s shocked diabetes researchers—they discovered that some people with maturity-onset diabetes have insulin circulating in their blood. This discovery meant that diabetes could not be due *only* to the absence of insulin in the body, and sparked a major rethinking of attitudes toward the nature and causes of the disease. The result: new approaches to the treatment of diabetes. The test is also being studied as an indicator of the presence of latent diabetes, and is making it possible to discover the disease before any symptoms appear.

Scientists have been looking for other sensitive tests that will permit them to diagnose diabetics *before* they come down with serious symptoms of the disease. If such susceptible people can be identified, early treatment with diet control might prevent the breakdown of the beta cells and thus eliminate all the problems of the actual disease. Researchers have been seeking markers that might identify such individuals, and have eagerly followed up a number of leads. They have tried testing for the presence of synalbumin in the blood (synalbumin is a protein that can inactivate insulin); for the presence of larger than normal amounts of zinc in the urine (known diabetics often have this symptom); for a thickening of certain tissues in the blood vessels (another symptom diabetics, and prediabetics, often have). Unfortunately, none of these has proved a sure key to the risk of diabetes.

Scientists are also working to develop a sensitive test for antibodies against beta cells, which would help to predict juvenile diabetes. Another test now being perfected measures the level of a certain type of hemoglobin, the chemical that carries oxygen in the blood. This fraction, called hemoglobin A_{1C}, is present in larger amounts in diabetics than in normal people; the more of it there is, the severer the diabetes. The hemoglobin A_{1C} level changes slowly over a period of several weeks, rather than fluctuating during the day as the blood sugar level does. One test for hemoglobin A_{1C} could thus be used to screen people for diabetes, and to determine how effectively a treatment is controlling a diabetic condition.

Researchers are also working on a screening test for diabetes that involves a study of the way insulin and glucagon bind to the hormone receptors on the surface of cells. Some researchers claim that the cells of diabetics (and prediabetics) bind less insulin than normal cells.

How Diabetes Is Treated

Fads come and go. Hemlines of fashionable clothes go up or down from one year to the next. A generation ago a hula hoop craze swept across the nation, but the hula hoop was quickly forgotten as people began skimming Frisbees through the air as a form of spare-time fun. Science and medicine have had their own fads and fashions, and the treatment of diabetes is no exception.

Before Banting and Best isolated insulin and used it successfully to treat diabetic patients, the only effective treatment doctors had for diabetes was a carefully controlled diet. In the wave of enthusiasm that swept through the medical world after the insulin discovery, diet was almost forgotten. Diabetics still had to count calories, because a dose of insulin must balance the amount of food a diabetic eats if it is to keep the blood sugar in check. But the feeling grew that diet wasn't really that important—a diabetic who ate a little extra could cover it with a little more insulin. Then, when oral hypoglycemic drugs were discovered, many doctors and patients eagerly jumped on the bandwagon and began to use the new drugs. Now the fashions in diabetes treatment seem to have come full circle. The current feeling is that although insulin and oral hypoglycemic drugs can be useful in some cases, diet is of prime importance, and some patients can best be treated with a carefully controlled diet alone.

Diabetes is a rather unusual disease. In most types of illness, the doctor is completely in charge of the treatment. He or she prescribes the medicines and their doses, and may even give them by injections. Usually all the patient has to do is take some pills at specified times and follow any other instructions, such as staying in bed or drinking plenty of liquids. And most diseases have a limited course—after a few days, or weeks, or months, a person has recovered and no longer has the disease. But diabetes is a *chronic* disease: once started, it continues for the rest of the person's life. Through all this time it must be actively treated on a day-to-day basis.

Very few people could afford to have a doctor living with them and treating them every day. Even if all diabetics could afford this, there would not be enough doctors to go around. So the diabetic must act as a sort of "assistant doctor" in charge of the day-to-day management of his or her own case—running tests, working out doses, and even giving injections. Fortunately, the modern treatments for diabetes are simple enough that they can be mastered by anyone who is willing to practice a few techniques and learn a bit about the disease. (Some diabetics become so interested that they eventually learn more about diabetes than many doctors know!) Periodically, of course, the diabetic sees a doctor for tests of how well the treatment is going. And the doctor is always available for emergency calls if special problems come up.

Most people don't much like the idea of going to a doctor for "shots," and the idea of having one or more injections every day (and giving them to *yourself*!) might seem like torture. But a person quickly loses the fear of injections when they are given frequently, and daily insulin shots soon become a routine.

Giving yourself an injection is really not too hard to do, and diabetic patients as young as four years old have been taught to do it properly. First, you fill the syringe to the proper dose from the insulin bottle, taking care that no air bubbles remain in the syringe. Then you wipe a spot on the skin with a cotton swab dipped in alcohol; this cleans the skin and kills any germs that might otherwise slip into the body and cause an infection. Then, with one hand, you pinch up the skin into a bulge. (In a muscular area like the thigh, it may be better to stretch the skin out tight rather than pinch it.) You quickly insert the needle into the skin. (The quicker you are, the less it hurts.) You pull the plunger back a little, to make sure the needle is not entering a blood vessel. (The insulin should be absorbed slowly from the tissues, rather than shot all at once into the bloodstream.) Then you push the plunger down, injecting all the insulin in the syringe; withdraw the needle carefully; and wipe the skin again with alcohol. If you used a plastic disposable syringe, it is thrown away. Otherwise, you wash the syringe carefully and sterilize it by boiling. (Bacteria could multiply on a dirty syringe, so reusing it without taking these precautions could be dangerous.)

The places on the body most often used for insulin injections are the belly, buttocks, thighs, and upper arms. (An injection in the arm may have to be given by someone else.) Diabetics rotate their injections among the various parts of the body, never giving an injection in exactly the same spot more than once a month. There are two reasons for this. Too many injections in the same spot in quick succession can make the skin and tissues sensitive and sore. In addition, insulin injections sometimes cause the fat deposits under the skin to be absorbed into the body, causing an unsightly dent in the flesh. This effect can usually be avoided by not injecting insulin into the same place more than once every few weeks.

How do you know how much insulin to inject? The doctor sets the doses and the routine of the injections after a period of trial and gradual adjustment. (The aim is to use the smallest amount of insulin that will keep the blood sugar under good control.) Then the diabetic may make minor changes in the dose on the basis of daily urine tests and any changes in his or her schedule, or special stress, that may arise. A cold or some more serious illness will make the body require more insulin, while heavy exercise will burn up sugar and decrease a diabetic's insulin requirement. (In fact, a diabetic may need to take some sugar before exercise—for example, a candy bar or soft drink before gym.)

Diabetics have discovered that if some particularly vigorous exercise is planned—some fast sets of tennis, for instance—it is a good idea not to inject insulin into a muscle that will be working hard. That would cause the insulin to be absorbed much faster than usual and give the effect of an overdose. So, before a game of tennis or basketball, the best place to inject insulin would be the belly, rather than the arms or thighs.

Several types of insulin are used, either separately or in combinations, to treat diabetic patients. *Regular insulin* is a pure form of insulin, sometimes called "plain," "clear," or "unmodified." It is quick-acting but doesn't last long. It starts working within half an hour to an hour, has the greatest effect in two to three hours, and is all gone within four to six hours.

In 1936 a Danish researcher, D. H. C. Hagedorn, discovered that if insulin is combined with prot-amine, a protein obtained from fish sperm, it is absorbed more slowly and steadily into the blood. *NPH insulin* (the letters stand for "neutral protamine Hage-dorn"), also called *Isophane insulin*, is a milky white suspension of tiny crystals, which must be mixed thoroughly before use. It is a fairly long-acting insulin. It begins working in two to four hours, has its greatest effect in eight to twelve hours, and is all gone in twenty to twenty-four hours.

Semilente insulin begins to work as quickly as Regular insulin, but its effects last longer—up to eight hours; it has its peak in two to four hours. *Ultralente insulin* is a very slow-acting form; it takes six to eight hours to begin working and works for thirty-six hours. *Lente insulin* is a combination of Semilente and Ultralente; it starts working within two to four hours and lasts for about twenty-four hours, with a peak at eight to twelve hours. (The name *lente* comes from the Italian word meaning slow.)

Regular insulin is the best type for emergencies, when quick action is needed to bring a person out of diabetic coma. But for daily use it is often rather inconvenient, at least by itself—since it lasts such a short time, a number of injections a day would be needed. (Nevertheless, there are some diabetics for whom the best treatment is several injections of Regular insulin every day.) Some of the longer-acting insulins do last over a whole day, and a single injection first thing in the morning may be enough to keep the blood sugar under control. But these insulins begin acting so slowly that they could not prevent serious sugar spills if a diabetic ate a meal at a time when the insulin's action was not at its peak. Increasing the dose to cover an early meal would mean that at its peak the insulin's action would be *too* high, and the person might go into insulin shock. Doctors get around these problems by using mixtures of insulin—for example, Regular with NPH insulin, or combinations of Lente with Regular or Semilente; often such a mixture is used in each of two daily injections.

The size and timing of meals are very important for a diabetic taking insulin. A healthy pancreas adjusts the amount of insulin it delivers to the body's needs. A large meal or a high-calorie dessert will call for a stepped-up flow of insulin. If a healthy person skips a meal, his or her pancreas will not secrete unneeded insulin. But a diabetic taking insulin is locked into a set pattern of insulin flow during the day. Once the injection is given, the amount of insulin available cannot be increased or decreased to meet changing needs. There will not be enough insulin to cope with an unexpectedly heavy meal or a high-calorie treat eaten on a whim, and the excess sugar will flood the blood and spill over into the urine. Skipping a meal, or even not eating as much as planned, will mean that there is not enough sugar in the blood to use up the injected insulin. Then the blood sugar level will fall—sometimes not to just a normal level, but to a hypoglycemic level, one far below normal. Soon sensitive brain cells will be affected by the sugar lack—without enough of their energy fuel, they cannot work properly.

A diabetic who has too much insulin in his or her blood may become tired and irritable. He or she may say irrational things, and, as the sugar level falls, may even act peculiarly, and might do things like taking off clothes in a public place. Feeling disoriented—not knowing where you are or how you got there—is a more common experience. "Feeling funny" and "acting different" can be the first signs of a low blood sugar reaction, or too much insulin. They are important warnings that can help the diabetic ward off the more serious effects of *insulin shock*. Diabetics taking insulin must be careful always to carry some sugar cubes, candy, or other source of quick-acting sugar. If sugar is taken, or given to the diabetic by his companions, at the first sign of developing insulin shock, the blood sugar level will rise, and a dangerous reaction will be prevented.

Diabetic coma, resulting from an extremely high blood sugar level, and insulin shock, resulting from a drastic fall in the blood sugar, are both very serious medical emergencies. If not treated promptly, they can kill. Their causes are opposite, and they require opposite treatments. But if a diabetic suddenly collapses, how can you tell whether he or she is suffering from diabetic coma or insulin shock? A life may depend on taking the right action. Yet the symptoms of the two conditions are sometimes confused. Here is how to tell them apart:

INSULIN REACTION	DIABETIC COMA
Starts suddenly	Develops gradually
Skin pale and moist	Skin dry and hot
Dizziness	No dizziness
Great hunger	Little hunger
Normal thirst	Extreme thirst
Shallow breathing	Deep, difficult breathing
Normal breath odor	Fruity (acetone) breath odor
Tongue moist	Tongue dry
Normal urination	Excessive urination
Confusion, strange behavior	Drowsiness, lethargy
No acetone in urine	Acetone in urine
Little or no sugar in urine	Large amounts of sugar in urine

If you are uncertain, the best thing to do is to treat for an insulin reaction. Insulin shock develops so rapidly that quick action may be needed to save the person's life or prevent brain damage. If it turns out that the person was really suffering from diabetic coma, a little more sugar is not going to make much difference, and since the condition develops more slowly, there will be time to correct for the mistake with injections of fast-acting insulin. Of course, if the person does not respond promptly to a dose of sugar, a doctor should be called. Medical help should be sought in any case if the person is unconscious.

If someone suffering from an insulin reaction is conscious, give him or her sugar lumps, candy, or sweetened orange juice or soft drinks (NOT diet soda!). This will bring recovery within minutes.

Never try to force any food or drink down the throat of an unconscious person—it might go into the windpipe and cause suffocation. (However, you could try putting honey or jam on your finger and placing the finger between the person's cheek and teeth.) An emergency injection of glucagon can help to bring a person out of a severe insulin reaction. A doctor might also give an intravenous injection of glucose. In any case, speed is important. The longer a person is unconscious with insulin shock before treatment is begun, the slower and less complete the recovery will be.

Regular injections of insulin provide reasonably good control for diabetics who make little or no insulin of their own. Insulin injections are the best treatment for juvenile diabetics, whose beta cells are damaged. However, other approaches can be successfully used for diabetics who make some insulin, but not enough to maintain a normal blood sugar level.

Some diabetics can keep their blood sugar level under control with oral hypoglycemic drugs. Most of those now in use belong to a group called the *sulfonylureas*. These drugs are chemically related to the sulfa drugs, although they do not possess the ability to kill bacteria. The first of the sulfonylureas to be marketed for the treatment of diabetes was tolbutamide. It was developed in Germany in 1954 and is sold in the United States under the trade name Orinase. Tolbutamide is not an insulin substitute. It works by stimulating the pancreas to increase its secretion of insulin. Thus, it is effective only in maturity-onset diabetes, in which the pancreas is still able to manufacture at least some insulin.

After tolbutamide, other sulfonylureas were developed for diabetes treatment; these include Diabinese (chlorpropamide), Dymelor (acetohexamide), and Tolinase (tolazamide). Diabinese and Tolinase are considerably more potent than tolbutamide, but, unfortunately, they are more likely to produce side effects. A far more potent sulfonylurea, glybenclamide, can be used in extremely small doses and does not seem to produce bad side effects. It is available throughout much of the world, but not in the United States.

Another type of oral antidiabetic drug that is

sometimes used is *phenformin*. It is not a sulfonylurea; it belongs to the chemical group of biguanides, part of a larger class of compounds called guanidines. Although phenformin came on the market after tolbutamide, the hypoglycemic effect of guanidines had actually been known since 1918. An unfortunate incident that occurred in 1926 cut off diabetes research on the guanidines for a while. A member of the guanidine family called Synthalin was promoted as an effective drug for lowering blood sugar levels. But it had been placed on the market too quickly, before enough tests had been run. Synthalin *was* an effective drug for lowering blood sugar levels, but doctors soon found that it damaged the livers of up to 40 percent of its users! When this was discovered, Synthalin was quickly taken off the market.

Phenformin does not damage the liver, but it does have other potentially serious side effects, so the drug is now available only by special prescription to patients who cannot take insulin and whose blood sugar levels cannot be kept under control without it.

In the late 1950s, when the oral antidiabetic drugs became available, many doctors and diabetics eagerly began using them. It seemed that they had been thoroughly tested for safety and effectiveness. Tolbutamide, for example, was tested on twenty thousand selected patients before the Food and Drug Administration (FDA) approved it for sale in the United States in 1957. Oral drugs were so much more convenient than insulin injections, or fussing over strict diets. But gradually doubts began to emerge.

In 1960 a major study called the University Group Diabetes Program (UGDP) was set up to try to resolve once and for all whether the new oral hypoglycemic drugs were really safe and effective. Large groups of diabetics at twelve university clinics in the United States and Puerto Rico were treated in one of the following ways: with diet alone; with insulin (either in fixed or in variable amounts); with tolbutamide; or with a placebo (an inactive substance that the patients were told was an active drug). Another group receiving phenformin was later added. The study went on for nearly ten years; then, when the results were announced, the storm broke.

The UGDP findings indicated that diabetics treated with oral antidiabetic drugs had a much higher risk of dying from heart attacks than patients in any of the other groups had—twice as high, in fact. In addition, the drugs didn't seem to be so effective after all. The diabetics treated with only a restriction of diet showed just as good a control of their blood sugar levels as the diabetics receiving the drugs. Even the results with placebos seemed about the same. (Apparently some diabetics can control their blood sugar if they *think* they are receiving a drug that will do it!) When diabetics were taken off the oral drugs, their conditions stayed about the same—or sometimes even improved.

What a howl the announcement provoked. Frightened diabetics called their doctors asking what to do. Some doctors immediately stopped prescribing oral antidiabetic drugs and switched their patients to other forms of treatment. But some diabetes specialists who had had good results with the drugs questioned the UGDP findings. They analyzed the study and decided that it had not been well designed. These doctors said that some of the patients receiving the oral drugs shouldn't have been receiving them at all, since they had mild forms of diabetes that could easily have been controlled by diet. The differences in results, they claimed, were not really significant. And not enough precautions had been taken to rule out the possibility that the people in the drug groups just happened to be more heart attack–prone in the first place. Other diabetes experts maintained that the UGDP studies *were* valid and cited results of other studies that confirmed what the UGDP had found. They also pointed out that the drugs may work well for a while, but that eventually the increased insulin levels they stimulate produce a decrease in the number of insulin receptors on the surface of body cells and thus make the cells more insulin-resistant.

The controversy raged on, fueled by a new UGDP report that insulin injections did not seem to be significantly more effective in treating maturity-onset diabetes than treatment with diet alone. While one group of diabetes specialists fought in the courts, trying to get all the records of the UGDP study released for examination, some of the doctors who had participated in the study examined the data they had available and found some glaring flaws. Deaths of patients were tabulated according to the treatment group to which they had been assigned; yet in some cases the diabetics had never actually received the treatment they were supposedly getting. Patients listed as receiving insulin had been treated with diet alone; some in the oral drug treatment groups had actually received insulin; and so forth. The patients in the study were supposed to be healthy except for their diabetes; yet one clinic had recruited volunteers from a heart disease clinic—so how could it be said that a particular diabetes treatment had contributed to deaths from heart disease? Some deaths in the placebo group were not included in the statistical analysis—so perhaps it wasn't true after all that placebos were about as effective as the oral hypoglycemic drugs.

The FDA launched a massive audit of the UGDP project. The auditors found "errors and discrepancies," but concluded that there were not enough of them to change the basic findings of the study. The results of the audit were nevertheless challenged by diabetes specialists whose own analyses led to quite different conclusions. Amid charges of cover-ups and cries of "medical Watergate," the UGDP affair has developed into a major medical scandal.

Where did all this leave the puzzled physician, trying to treat his diabetic patients according to the best accepted medical wisdom? Gradually, a commonsense philosophy of diabetes management has emerged. Diabetes specialists now advise that a doctor first try to treat a maturity-onset diabetic with a controlled diet, especially if he or she is overweight. If that does not work, a program of insulin treatment should be tried. (Insulin may also be necessary at the beginning of the treatment program, to relieve severe symptoms, even in a case in which it is eventually possible to change to a program of diet alone.) Only if good control is *not* obtained with insulin, or if the diabetic cannot take insulin for some reason, should oral antidiabetic drugs be tried, either alone or in combination with insulin or other drugs.

Some diabetes specialists now feel that the worst thing about the oral antidiabetic drugs is that they falsely lull people (both doctors and patients) into believing that the control of diabetes is easy, and that worrying about diet and strict control of blood sugar is unnecessary. For the diabetic, diet *is* important, and keeping the blood sugar level as close as possible to normal can help to prevent many of the complications of diabetes, such as arteriosclerosis, nerve damage, and diabetic retinopathy.

What is the "right" diet for a diabetic? That is a question that has been debated for thousands of years, and even now medical experts do not all agree. Some very odd-sounding variations of diet have been tried, even within the past few decades; these include a diet of nothing but oatmeal, and a diet of apples and rice. For a long time the accepted wisdom in treating diabetics was that they should avoid sugars completely and other carbohydrates as much as possible. That left a diet high in proteins and fats, and very low in natural fiber. Unless calories are counted very strictly, such a diet can lead to a gain in weight, and large amounts of animal fats in the diet are thought to contribute to heart disease. Most doctors now believe that a diet high in protein and fat and very low in carbohydrate is not a very good diet for diabetics after all.

The diet now recommended for diabetics contains moderate amounts of carbohydrates (including foods with plenty of natural fiber, such as fruits and whole-grain cereals) and proteins, and a rather small amount of fat. Animal fats should be kept to a minimum; so should refined sugars, such as table sugar, which pass quickly into the blood. The *amount* of food a diabetic eats is particularly important, both for diabetics taking insulin and for those being treated with diet alone. There should be enough food in the diet to provide nourishment, but not enough to cause weight gain (except in actively growing children). Obese diabetics need a diet that will help them to lose weight, for often lowering the weight to normal will decrease or even eliminate the need for any other therapy.

Dividing the day's food into four or five meals places less of a load on the pancreas than eating two or three large meals. And, for a person taking insulin, a number of small meals helps to even out the day's insulin requirement and avoid the danger of a between-meals insulin reaction. Eating a large number of meals each day has also been recommended as a means of losing weight. Of course, this works only if you take the proper amount of food and divide it into a larger number of meals per day—if you eat three regular-sized meals and add two or three snacks a day, you will just gain weight.

In the past few years, the medical world has been rediscovering fiber, also called "roughage" or "bulk in the diet." Plants contain a great deal of cellulose fiber, which humans cannot digest. Cows, rabbits, and other plant-eating animals digest cellulose with the aid of bacteria that live in their digestive tracts. For them, cellulose is a source of sugar, but for us it is just indigestible "roughage" that passes out of the body unchanged. Dietary fiber helps to keep the bowels moving regularly, and recent studies indicate that it may be helpful in preventing heart disease and some types of cancer. Studies of diabetics given a high-fiber diet have shown that their blood sugar levels were lowered. Those who were taking insulin became less dependent on it, and the dose could be reduced. (The fiber was provided in the form of raw fruits, vegetables, and nuts, or in the form of supplements such as bran.)

Diabetics, like everyone else, should eat a nutritious, well-balanced diet. But many people do not know very much about nutrition, and they are unsure about which foods they should eat, and how much of them. So helpful diet plans for diabetics have been drawn up. Many of them provide a great deal of latitude for indulging personal preferences in foods. These diet plans operate on the basis of "exchanges"—portions of foods that are equivalent in type and amount of nourishment. Some foods that might seem equivalent are not. For example, bread exchanges and fruit exchanges both contain carbohydrates. But one cannot be substituted for the other, because fruits contain sugars that are quickly absorbed into the bloodstream, producing a rapid rise in the blood sugar level, while bread contains starches, which must be broken down into sugars and are therefore absorbed more slowly. Substitutions may be made within exchange groups, however. For example, a diabetic might eat a portion of cereal or spaghetti instead of bread. Amounts of fruit, bread, milk, meat, and fat are limited in a typical diabetic diet, but most green vegetables are on a "free" list. You can eat as much of them as you like, because they are very low in carbohydrates and calories, and high in fiber.

The problems of diets for diabetics have been at the center of the recent controversy over saccharin, an artificial sweetener that is commonly substituted for sugar. Some studies have indicated that saccharin may increase users' risk of cancer. Normally, when a food additive is found to be cancer-causing, it is immediately removed from the market. But when the FDA tried to do this with saccharin, it was flooded with complaints.

Some scientists say that the saccharin studies are not conclusive, and point to the fact that many people have been taking saccharin for forty or fifty years without any apparent ill effects. Others say that *any*

BREAD EXCHANGES

1 exchange contains about 15 grams C, 2 grams P, and 70 calories

baked beans, ¼ cup
biscuit, 2-inch
bread, 1 slice
cereal, cooked, ½ cup
cereal, dry, ¾ cup
corn, ⅓ cup
graham crackers, 2
macaroni, ½ cup
muffin, 2-inch
noodles, ½ cup
popcorn, 1 cup
potato, small
rice, ½ cup
saltine crackers, 5
spaghetti, ½ cup
sweet potatoes, ¼ cup

FAT EXCHANGES

1 exchange contains about 5 grams F and 45 calories

bacon, 1 slice
butter, 1 teaspoon
cream, heavy, 1 tablespoon
cream, light, 2 tablespoons
cream cheese, 1 tablespoon
French dressing, 1 tablespoon
margarine, 1 teaspoon
mayonnaise, 1 teaspoon
oil, 1 teaspoon
olives, 5 small
nuts, 6 small

FRUIT EXCHANGES

1 exchange contains about 10 grams C and 40 calories

apple, small
applesauce, ½ cup
banana, one half
blackberries, ¾ cup
blueberries, ¾ cup
cantaloupe, one quarter
cherries, 10 large
grapefruit, one half
grapefruit juice, ½ cup
grapes, 12 average
orange, small
orange juice, ½ cup
peach, medium
pear, small
pineapple, ½ cup
plums, 2 medium
raisins, 2 tablespoons
raspberries, ¾ cup
strawberries, 1 cup
tangerine, large
watermelon, 1 cup

MILK EXCHANGES

1 exchange contains about 12 grams C, 8 grams P, 10 grams F, and 170 calories

buttermilk, 1 cup
evaporated milk, ½ cup
skim milk, 1 cup
whole milk, 1 cup

MEAT EXCHANGES

1 exchange = 1 ounce, unless otherwise noted

1 exchange contains about 7 grams P, 5 grams F, and 75 calories

American cheese
beef
bologna, 1 slice
cheddar cheese
chicken
clams, 5 small
codfish
cottage cheese, ¼ cup
egg, large
flounder
frankfurter, 2-ounce
haddock
lamb
liver
liverwurst, 1 slice
oysters, 5 small
peanut butter, 2 tablespoons *
perch
pork
salami, 1 slice
sardines, 3 medium
shrimp, 5 small
Swiss cheese
tunafish, ¼ cup
turkey
veal

*Peanut butter also contains carbohydrate, and should be limited to 1 exchange a day.

VEGETABLE EXCHANGES
(List A)

1 exchange = ½ cup

1 exchange contains about 7 grams C, 2 grams P, and 35 calories

beets
carrots
green peppers
onions
peas
turnips

"FREE" VEGETABLES
(List B)

¾-cup portion contains little C, P, or F, and few calories

asparagus
broccoli
brussels sprouts
cabbage
cauliflower
celery
cucumbers
lettuce
mushrooms
radishes
sauerkraut
spinach
string beans
tomatoes, tomato juice
wax beans

These are typical lists of the different kinds of food "exchanges." In planning menus, a diabetic may "exchange" any item in one list for any other item in the same list.

The number of grams of carbohydrate (C), protein (P), and fat (F) in each kind of exchange is given because doctors and diabetics use these values to help them plan balanced diets.

	grams of carbohydrate	grams of protein	grams of fat	calories
7 bread exchanges	105	14		490
4 fat exchanges			20	180
4 fruit exchanges	40			160
3 milk exchanges	36	24	30	510
7 meat exchanges		49	35	525
3 vegetable exchanges (from List A)	21	6		105
2 (or more) vegetables from List B				—
TOTALS	202	93	85	1,970

SAMPLE MENUS FOR ONE DAY

Breakfast
    ½ cup orange juice
    2 pieces of toast
    2 teaspoons butter
    1 egg
    1 cup milk

Midmorning snack
    2 tablespoons raisins

Lunch
    sandwich made with 2 slices of bread,
        1 teaspoon mayonnaise,
        2 slices bologna,
        lettuce
    carrot sticks
    1 cup milk
    2 plums

Afternoon snack
    tomato juice
    5 saltine crackers

Dinner
    4 ounces roast beef
    ⅔ cup corn
    salad with 1 tablespoon French dressing
    celery sticks
    carrot sticks
    ½ cup peas
    1 cup milk
    ½ cup applesauce

The 1,970-calorie diet outlined at the top of the page is one a doctor might prescribe for a youthful diabetic who is not overweight. The sample menus show how the diabetic following this diet might choose to eat his or her daily allotment of food.

risk of cancer is too much risk, and it is better not to take the chance. The opinions of diabetics and the doctors who treat and study them have also been mixed. Some doctors feel that diabetics shouldn't use saccharin, that it simply maintains their "sweet tooth." If diabetics tried eating a more sensible diet, these doctors say, they would soon lose their taste for rich, sweet foods, and that would be a good thing. But some diabetics feel that life just wouldn't be worth living if they couldn't have candy, a soft drink, or some other sweet-tasting treat at least occasionally. And some doctors feel that saccharin is good in that it permits diabetics, especially young diabetics, to enjoy some of the same treats as healthy people, which can help them feel less "different." Fortunately, researchers are working to develop other no-calorie sweeteners, and there may soon be safe replacements for saccharin.

Living with Diabetes

It is a shock to be told that you have diabetes. Even after you get over the first worries over whether you will live or die, there are great adjustments to make. A life of restrictions seems to stretch out ahead, with no end or letup in sight. What will you be allowed to eat? Will you be able to work and play like other people? What about marriage and raising a family? Will you be able to master the techniques of giving insulin injections and counting calories? How much of a dent will they make in the normal routines of living?

For most diabetics, the disease need not make that much of a change in their way of life. Active living is not only possible but desirable for a diabetic. Exercise helps to lower the blood sugar level, and active interests in life keep a person from brooding about a chronic health problem.

Many famous people have lived with diabetes and not let it bother them. Statesmen and world leaders such as Georges Clemenceau, Mao Tse-tung, Francisco Franco, and Gamal Abdel Nasser were diabetic, as is Menachem Begin. Diabetes is no bar to a career in literature or the arts: British writer H. G. Wells, French artist Paul Cézanne, and Italian composer

Giacomo Puccini were diabetic. Diabetic stars in the world of show business include television personalities Dan Rowan and Mary Tyler Moore. Taking daily insulin injections need not stop a career in sports. Ice hockey superstar Bobby Clarke has had juvenile diabetes since the age of fifteen. Baseball stars Ron Santo and Catfish Hunter are diabetic too. Tennis star William Talbert won twenty-five national tennis titles and twenty world championships; as captain of the U.S. Davis Cup team, he traveled more than five million miles, giving himself daily insulin injections wherever he went—for he had been a diabetic since the age of ten.

Some diabetics are reluctant to tell others about their condition, feeling that it is embarrassing and somehow shameful. Such fears are blown up out of proportion. Very few people would feel any different about you, knowing you were a diabetic, and most would be sympathetic and helpful. If you are taking insulin, it is important for at least one close friend to know about your condition and to know what to do to help you in case of an insulin reaction.

Wearing a medical identification bracelet or necklace or carrying an identification card can also be helpful in case of an emergency. Readily available information on your illness and what to do in case of insulin reaction or diabetic coma, as well as your name and the name and number of someone to contact, may mean the difference between life and death if you are found unconscious. A nonprofit organization, Medic–Alert Foundation, can provide you with an identification card or tag, and maintains a central file containing vital information on every case registered with it. This information can be obtained twenty-four hours a day by a collect telephone call.

Should diabetics marry? Can they hope to raise families of their own? Marriage to a diabetic requires some adjustments. (So does marriage to anyone!) They are adjustments that many people have made successfully. It is a matter of being willing to make the effort. Certainly the person a diabetic is planning to marry should know about his or her condition beforehand, and the couple should have frank and open discussions about what the treatment of the disease entails, and the possibility that complications might develop in the future.

Should diabetics marry each other? In the days when it was thought that juvenile diabetes was inherited by a simple recessive gene, the answer was usually a resounding *No*, since it was thought that any children the couple had would have a 100-percent chance of inheriting the disease. (Most young diabetics thinking of getting married and having children have juvenile, rather than maturity-onset, diabetes.) But now that studies have indicated that heredity does not play as significant a role in this form of the disease as was formerly thought, there doesn't seem to be much reason to discourage marriages between diabetics. In fact, some counselors who have worked with diabetics suggest that if two diabetics marry each other, they will find it easier to adjust, since both of them already know what living with the disease involves.

What about children? There is no reason why a diabetic man should not father a child. If a woman is diabetic, the problem is a bit more complicated. Modern methods of treating diabetes have greatly increased the chances for a diabetic woman to bear a normal, healthy child. But the rate of death of babies, both before and soon after birth, is still somewhat higher for diabetic mothers than for normal women. Diabetes itself also becomes more difficult to control during pregnancy—the body's need for insulin increases, and the woman must be carefully watched by her doctor to avoid possible complications that might threaten her or her child. A pregnant diabetic woman must often undergo frequent and costly blood tests and other tests to determine how well her baby is growing and when it should be delivered.

What about work? Some occupations, such as piloting an airplane or driving a bus, may not be open to diabetics, especially those who are taking insulin. These restrictions are imposed for safety reasons. Many people's lives might be endangered if a diabetic suddenly became unconscious in the cockpit or the driver's seat. But with relatively few exceptions, a diabetic is free to take up any occupation he or she wishes.

Insurance companies used to refuse to write life insurance policies on diabetics, which made sense when a person who was diagnosed as a diabetic generally died within a few years. But modern treatments have permitted most diabetics to live a nearly normal life, and insurance companies have changed with the times. Now life insurance policies are available for diabetics, although they may be charged somewhat higher rates than healthy people.

Can you travel if you're a diabetic? Certainly. Just make sure you take adequate supplies of insulin, syringes, urine testing materials, and any other paraphernalia you need. Modern insulin preparations will keep well at room temperature for a month or more, though they should be protected from extremes of heat and cold. (Never ship insulin supplies in the baggage compartment of an airplane, which may become boiling hot or freezing cold.) If you plan to visit a foreign country, it is a good idea to know how to say important phrases like "I am a diabetic" and "I need a doctor" in the language of the land, even if you can't say anything else. Another good precaution is to take along a doctor's note stating that you are a diabetic and must carry injection equipment to treat your condition—otherwise you might be suspected of being a drug addict or pusher and wind up in jail.

The routines a diabetic must follow can complicate his or her social life. Sticking to a strict diet can be hard, especially when you are at a party or out on a date. The insulin routine imposes additional problems, since you can't miss or even delay a meal. There are ways of getting around such problems gracefully, though. For instance, if you know that dinner will be served late or there will be a long delay in service at a restaurant, you can take a little snack beforehand to keep your insulin satisfied. (Be sure to deduct any extra calories from your meal later.) And it is possible to avoid overeating without hurting the cook's feelings. As long as you eat at least a little of a special dish, compliment your host or hostess, and say something like "I really wish I could eat more," the requirements of courtesy will be satisfied.

What about drinking? Some doctors say diabetics should drink no alcohol. Others permit a drink or two. But drinking has some special pitfalls for the diabetic. First of all, alcohol has calories, and they count in the diet. In addition, drinking tends to decrease a person's control, and after a drink or two, chatting with pleasant company, one may forget that a meal was due. A person who is "high" may not be alert to the signs of low blood sugar, and a full-blown insulin reaction may develop. Imagine being found on the street unconscious, with the smell of alcohol on your breath. Anyone who found you would be much more likely to call the police to cart you off to the drunk tank than to suspect you were suffering from insulin shock. Diabetics have died that way.

What about smoking? (That is a rather ambiguous word these days. We once had a conversation with a friend from New York City about our respective teenage children's attitudes toward smoking, and it was ten minutes before we realized that we were talking about smoking tobacco, but she was talking about smoking marijuana.) Cigarettes have been linked with so many damaging effects on the heart, lungs, and other systems of the body that acquiring the habit of smoking them is not a very good idea for anyone. It is an even worse idea for diabetics, who are in danger of developing damage to their circulatory systems anyway. As for marijuana, it, like alcohol, can dull your judgment and make you forget about eating a meal or taking an insulin injection. Or it may make you so hungry that you forget to stick to your diet.

Personal hygiene is particularly important for a diabetic—especially good care of the feet. The joys of walking around barefoot are not for the diabetic; it is too easy to get a cut or scratch that way. Diabetes can cause nerve damage that blunts the sense of touch, so one might not realize he or she had been injured, and the cut or scratch might become infected. The impaired healing of wounds that is characteristic of uncontrolled diabetes may lead to gangrene, and eventually the injured foot or leg might have to be amputated. (Such problems usually develop in older diabetics, rather than young people.) Progress is being made in treating diabetic foot problems, but diabetes is still the leading cause of amputation of limbs.

Getting sick can present special problems for a diabetic. The stress of an illness can make diabetes symptoms worse—and a diabetic condition can make the illness worse. A diabetic's doctor should be alerted whenever he or she gets sick; urine tests may have to be taken every few hours and the insulin dosage continually readjusted to help keep the blood sugar under control.

Recovering from an accident can also increase a diabetic's insulin requirements, and often, after an accident, a diabetic needs special care until he or she has gotten completely well.

Are all the special adjustments a diabetic must make worth it? For most diabetics, they are. Eating a sensible, well-balanced diet, getting plenty of exercise, and taking other commonsense health measures that are really good for everyone can make it possible for most diabetics to live a long and healthy life. And there is hope that some of the diabetes research going on in laboratories today may bring better methods of control—and real *cures*—in the future.

Frontiers of Diabetes Research

What is wrong with today's diabetes treatments? One main problem is that often they don't control the blood sugar level well enough. A normal pancreas sends out insulin only when it is needed, and in the precise amounts needed. But insulin injections provide a fixed amount of insulin, regardless of the body's actual needs. So the diabetic's blood sugar level bounces up and down, depending on how well the insulin supply happens to match the needs of the moment. George Cahill, president of the American Diabetes Association and a professor of medicine at Harvard University, has said that trying to control glucose metabolism with insulin injections is like trying to run a refrigerator without a thermostat by setting the cooler to run fifteen or twenty minutes each hour, regardless of whether the machine is too hot or too cold. Many of the current research efforts in the field of diabetes are aimed at devising ways to come closer to the sensitive natural methods of control that the healthy body uses.

An even more basic problem with modern techniques of diabetes control is that we are still treating symptoms, not causes. Studies of how the pancreas and its hormones work, and the many reactions of carbohydrate metabolism, may lead to better methods of intervening to correct mistakes in these processes. Only with this kind of basic knowledge can we hope to discover real *cures* for diabetes.

Somatostatin has been one major focus of diabetes research efforts. This hormone, discovered by a research team at the Salk Institute in 1972, has been found to have many effects. It inhibits the secretion of a number of hormones, including growth hormone, insulin, glucagon, the kidney hormone renin, and several hormones that affect the organs of digestion. It also decreases the production of certain digestive juices, the transmission of messages along nerves, and the clotting of blood. (This last effect produced internal bleeding in some experimental animals that received doses of the hormone.)

Obviously, somatostatin itself has too many side effects to be used as an antidiabetic drug, even though it does effectively lower the blood sugar level. Researchers are tinkering with the chemical structure of the hormone, which is a rather simple protein-like substance containing only fourteen amino acids. (Insulin, with fifty-one amino acids, is considered a small protein.) Some variations with more selective action than somatostatin have already been produced. But these, like somatostatin itself, are active for just a few minutes—not long enough to be of any help in controlling diabetes. Other variations of somatostatin that act for up to eight hours have been produced—

for example, by combining the hormone with zinc and protamine. (This is the same approach that was used to make longer-acting insulin.) Studies are continuing to try to find a variation of the hormone with the best combination of selective effect and long action. In other studies, researchers are trying to work out just how somatostatin acts, so that perhaps drugs to increase the body's production of it may be made.

In another investigation of how the diabetes process works, researchers discovered that, in maturity-onset diabetes, a *prostaglandin* seems to inhibit insulin secretion by the pancreas. (Prostaglandins are hormone-like substances.) This prostaglandin apparently prevents the pancreas from recognizing the signals of a rise in the blood sugar level. Scientists already knew that the common drug aspirin relieves pain and swelling by acting against another prostaglandin. So they tried injecting sodium salicylate, a chemical very closely related to aspirin, into the blood of maturity-onset diabetics to see if it would counteract the effect of the prostaglandin that reduces insulin secretion. Such treatment increased the flow of insulin from the pancreas and lowered the diabetics' blood sugar levels. Curiously enough, aspirin was used to treat diabetes in Germany more than a century ago, with some success. But after insulin became readily available, the German studies were forgotten.

In 1977, drug researchers at the McNeil Company announced promising test results of a new oral antidiabetic drug, McN–4359, that is not related chemically to either the sulfonylureas or the guanidines, has none of their side effects, and seems to be far more potent. The new drug is related to a family of drugs that have been effective in treating diseases of the heart and blood vessels.

As the mechanisms of some of the complications of diabetes have been worked out, scientists have begun to devise new ways to prevent their development. One team at the University of Maryland is looking for ways to prevent the formation of sorbitol, which accumulates in the eyes when the blood sugar level is high and can lead to blindness. A key enzyme in the chain of reactions that converts glucose to sorbitol is called *aldose reductase*. The Maryland researchers have found that some of the *flavonoids*, compounds found widely in plants, can block the action of aldose reductase. Now the group is looking for variations that are more potent and more stable than natural flavonoids, and would be suitable to use as eye drops.

Neuropathy, the progressive nerve damage that plagues some diabetics, is another complication that may be more preventable now that more is known about its chemical mechanisms. High levels of glucose in the blood result in a loss of myoinositol from the nerves. (Remember that myoinositol is a chemical nerves need to function.) University of Alabama researchers think that eating a diet high in myoinositol can help to prevent nerve damage due to diabetes. Cantaloupes, peanuts, grapefruit, and whole-grain cereals are all rich in myoinositol.

Several lines of study are aimed at making methods of insulin treatment more effective. Scientists at a number of laboratories are working on ways to produce synthetic insulin cheaply—even synthetic human insulin. One of the most exciting approaches makes use of the new recombinant DNA techniques.

DNA is the chemical of heredity, the substance in our genes in which the blueprints for all the structures and functions of the body are spelled out in a chemically coded form. There is a gene for making each protein in the body, including a gene for making insulin. (The hormone is actually produced first in a larger, inactive form called *proinsulin*, which is then split when there is a need for insulin secretion.) Other living organisms, even microscopic bacteria and viruses, have their own genes.

Recently scientists have learned how to isolate small rings of bacterial DNA called *plasmids*, split them, and insert genes from other organisms. (This "recombining" of DNA from different organisms gives the recombinant DNA technique its name.) Even genes from mammals—including humans—can be inserted into plasmids this way. Then the plasmid is introduced into a bacterium, and there the plasmid DNA, with its inserted gene, is faithfully copied, again and again. The bacterium grows and then divides, forming two new cells that are smaller copies of the original bacterium. Each new bacterial cell has its own copies of the changed plasmid. Since bacteria can divide as often as every twenty minutes, a single bacterium can quickly give rise to millions of off-spring. Though one bacterium is too small to be seen without a microscope, it would not take very long for pounds of its offspring to be produced. Theoretically, bacteria could thus be used to make pounds of any particular protein.

Early in 1978, a group of California researchers produced a bacterium containing a working gene for the hormone somatostatin. In June of the same year, researchers at Harvard University and the Joslin Diabetes Foundation in Boston announced that they had successfully used recombinant DNA techniques to get bacteria to produce a form of proinsulin according to the blueprint provided by the proinsulin gene from rats. Only a few months later, researchers at the City of Hope Medical Center in Duarte, California, announced that they had produced *human* insulin by recombinant DNA techniques.

Even with human insulin available, the problem would still remain: how can it be delivered the way the pancreas delivers it—only when it is needed, and in the amounts needed? One answer is to build an artificial pancreas. This machine would need to be sensitive to a rise in the blood sugar level, just like a real pancreas, and it would need to be able to measure out and deliver just the right amount of insulin to keep the sugar level within normal limits—all the time. Such a device would therefore have to include the following parts: a glucose sensor, which would detect glucose in the blood and measure its concentration; a refillable insulin reservoir; a pump to shoot measured microdoses of insulin into the body, and a power source to drive the pump; and a computer to make the responses of the artificial pancreas correspond precisely to the information gathered by the sensor.

All that machinery! It sounds as if it would take up a great deal of space. Some researchers working on the artificial pancreas have been concentrating on building a machine that does the job, without worrying about size. Toronto researchers Michael Albisser and Bernard Leibel have developed a bulky bedside machine, the Biostator, that can finely regulate blood sugar level. The machine is now being manufactured commercially by Miles Laboratories and is being used successfully in large hospitals to bring patients out of diabetic coma and quickly stabilize their glucose metabolism.

But a diabetic couldn't live a normal life dragging around a Biostator. For daily control, a tiny artificial pancreas that could be implanted into the body, as artificial heart pacemakers are, would be needed. We already have the technology to produce such a machine. For example, computer producers can make a tiny "brain" that fits onto a little silicon chip no bigger than a fingernail. Researchers at the Joslin Diabetes Foundation are designing an artificial pancreas about the size of a pack of cigarettes. A University of Southern California team has developed a glucose sensor about the size of a nickel, and a pump the size of a walnut, and are working on the computer circuits for another tiny, implantable device. Researchers in the USSR have also been working on an implantable artificial pancreas. Models have been tested on dogs and have even been tried in humans, although many technical problems still remain to be worked out.

People with failed kidneys and even hearts have been given new life with transplanted organs. What are the prospects of transplanting a healthy pancreas into a diabetic patient? In the rush of enthusiasm that followed the first successful heart transplants, surgeons tried transplanting a variety of other organs, including the pancreas. But nearly all the early pancreas transplants were unsuccessful, and doctors quickly realized that the problem was far more complicated than they had thought at first. One difficulty is that the pancreas produces not only hormones, but also fiercely active digestive juices. Drainage for these juices must be provided or they will cause trouble. And in any transplant operation there is the possibility of organ rejection. Organs from a body other than one's own are foreign tissues, and the body's immune system begins to make antibodies against them. Unless these immune responses are suppressed, the new organ will soon shrivel up and die. Unfortunately, the drugs that are usually used to suppress transplant rejection leave the patient without defenses against infections, and many transplant patients die of pneumonia or other infectious diseases. In addition, the immunosuppressive drugs tend to raise the blood sugar level, which would be particularly dangerous for someone already suffering from diabetes.

Recently, researchers have been concentrating on transplanting just the islet cells, rather than the whole pancreas. There have been some successes, generally in patients who have already had a kidney transplant and are taking immunosuppressive drugs. Studies in experimental animals have shown that islet cell transplants not only regulate the blood sugar level successfully, but even reverse some of the complications of diabetes, such as kidney damage.

One problem in islet cell transplants is getting enough cells for the operation. More than five hundred million cells are needed for a single transplant in a human being. One way around this difficulty is to grow the cells in tissue cultures for a while before transplanting them. Growing in laboratory dishes, the islet cells multiply without losing their ability to produce insulin in response to increased blood sugar levels; they also seem to change in some way, so that they are less likely to be rejected after they are transplanted into a diabetic's body.

Another way to get around the rejection problem may be to protect the islet cells from the patient's immune system. Joslin Diabetes Foundation researchers have cultured beta cells from newborn rats on bundles of artificial capillaries, thin tubes that allow small molecules to pass freely but hold back large particles. Sugar molecules could pass through the capillary walls into the islet cells, and insulin could pass out; but antibodies and white blood cells would be screened out. Researchers are now trying to devise materials for the capillaries that can be used safely and effectively in the body, so that "caged" islet cells can be implanted.

Experiments like these are opening new horizons in the treatment of diabetes and bringing new hope to diabetics all over the world.

For Further Information

Pamphlets and other helpful information on diabetes are provided by:

Juvenile Diabetes Foundation
23 East 26th Street
New York, New York 10010

American Diabetes Association, Inc.
1 West 48th Street
New York, New York 10020

Joslin Diabetes Foundation, Inc.
1 Joslin Place
Boston, Massachusetts 02215

People who make tax-deductible donations to the Juvenile Diabetes Foundation or to the Joslin Diabetes Foundation receive regular newsletters describing research highlights and giving practical information. The American Diabetes Association publishes a monthly magazine, *Forecast*.

* * *

A nonprofit organization, Medic–Alert Foundation, will provide you with an identification card or tag saying you are a diabetic (and listing any other health problems you may have) for a small one-time-only membership fee. The foundation also maintains a central file containing vital information on every case registered with it. This information can be obtained twenty-four hours a day by a collect telephone call. For details, write or phone:

> Medic–Alert Foundation International
> Turlock, California 95380
> Phone (209) 632-2371

*   *   *

Further information about diabetes can also be found in the following books:

FOR CHILDREN

Travis, Luther B. *An Instructional Aid on Juvenile Diabetes Mellitus*. 4th ed. Galveston, Texas: University of Texas Medical Branch, 1975.

FOR ADULTS

Biermann, June, and Toohey, Barbara. *The Diabetes Question and Answer Book*. Los Angeles: Sherbourne Press, 1974.

Brothers, Milton J. *Diabetes: The New Approach*. New York: Grosset and Dunlap, 1976.

Colwell, Arthur R. *Understanding Your Diabetes*. Springfield, Ill.: Charles C. Thomas, Publisher, 1978.

Court, John M. *Helping Your Diabetic Child*. New York: Taplinger Publishing Co., 1975.

Dolger, Henry, and Seeman, Bernard. *How to Live with Diabetes*. 4th ed. New York: W. W. Norton & Co., 1977.

Laufer, Ira J., and Kadison, Herbert. *Diabetes Explained: A Layman's Guide*. New York: E. P. Dutton & Co., 1976.

Index

ALVIN SILVERSTEIN grew up in Brooklyn, New York, and developed an early interest in science. He received his B.A. from Brooklyn College, his M.S. from the University of Pennsylvania, and his Ph.D. from New York University. He is Professor of Biology and Chairman of the Department of Biological Sciences at the College of Staten Island of the City University of New York.

VIRGINIA B. SILVERSTEIN, a native of Philadelphia, received her B.A. from the University of Pennsylvania. Since her marriage, she has worked as a free-lance translator of Russian scientific literature, doing extensive work for government and private agencies.

The Silversteins, who have collaborated on over fifty science books for young readers, live on a farm in Hunterdon County, New Jersey, with their six children.

DR. CHARLES NECHEMIAS is Assistant Clinical Professor of Medicine at The Mount Sinai School of Medicine of the City University of New York. He is also Assistant Attending Physician for Diabetes, and Physician to the Prenatal Diabetes Clinic, The Mount Sinai Hospital, New York.